GW00382850

Managing Products and Services

PS12

MARKETING

Published for
The National Examining Board for Supervisory Management

by
Pergamon Open Learning
a division of
Pergamon Press

Pergamon Press plc, Headington Hill Hall,
Oxford OX3 0BW, England

This unit supercedes the Super Series first edition unit 215, *Supervisors and Marketing* (first edition 1987)

Second edition 1991

A catalogue record for this book is available from the British Library

ISBN book and cassette kit: 0-08-041673-X

The views expressed in this work are those of the authors and do not necessarily reflect those of the National Examining Board for Supervisory Management or of the publisher.

Original text produced in conjunction with the Northern Regional Management Centre under an Open Tech Contract with the Manpower Services Commission.

Design and Production: Pergamon Open Learning

NEBSM Project Manager: Pam Sear
Author: Howard Senter
First Edition Author: David Johnson
Editor: Diana Thomas
Series Editor: Diana Thomas

Typeset by BPCC Techset Ltd, Exeter
Printed in Great Britain by BPCC Wheatons Ltd, Exeter

CONTENTS

1 Welcome to the User Guide

Hello and welcome to the NEBSM Super Series second edition (Super Series 2) flexible training programme.

It is quite likely that you are a supervisor, a team leader, an assistant manager, a foreman, a section head, a first-line or a junior manager and have people working under you. The Super Series programme is ideal for all, whatever the job title, who are on or near that first rung of the management ladder. By choosing this programme we believe that you have made exactly the right decision when it comes to meeting your own needs and those of your organization.

The purpose of this guide is to help you gain the maximum benefit both from this particular workbook and audio cassette and also from a full supervisory management training programme.

You should read the whole of this User Guide thoroughly before you start any work on the unit and use the information and advice to help plan your studies.

If you are are new to the idea of studying or training by yourself or have never before worked with a tutor or trainer on an individual basis, you should pay particular attention to the section below about Open Learning and tutorial support.

If you are a trainer or tutor evaluating this material for use with prospective students or clients, we think you will also find the information given here useful as it will help you to prepare and conduct individual pre-course counselling and group briefing sessions.

2 Your Open Learning Programme

What do we mean by 'Open Learning'?

Let's start by looking at what is meant by 'Open Learning' and how it could affect the way you approach your studies.

Open Learning is a term used to describe a method of training where you, the learner, make most of the decisions about *how*, *when* and *where* you do your learning. To make this possible you need to have available material, written or prepared in a special way (such as this book and audio cassette) and then have access to Open Learning centres that have been set up and prepared to offer guidance and support as and when required.

Undertaking your self-development training by Open Learning allows you to fit in with priorities at work and at home and to build the right level of confidence and independence needed for success, even though at first it may take you a little while to establish a proper routine.

The workbook and audio cassette

Though this guide is mainly aimed at you as a first time user, it is possible that you are already familiar with the earlier editions of the Super Series. If that is the case, you should know that there are quite a few differences in the workbook and audio cassette, some of which were very successfully trialled in the last 12 units of the first edition. Apart from the more noticeable features such as changes in page layouts and more extensive use of colour and graphics, you will find activities, questions and assignments that are more closely related to work and more thought-provoking.

The amount of material on the cassette is, on average, twice the length of older editions and is considerably more integrated with the workbook. In fact, there are so many extras now that are included as standard that the average study time per unit has been increased by almost a third. You will find a useful summary of all workbook and cassette features in the charts below and on page vii.

Whether you are a first time user or not, the first step towards being a successful Open Learner is to be familiar and comfortable with the learning material. It is well worth spending a little of your initial study time scanning the workbook to see how it is structured, what the various sections and features are called and what they are designed to do.

This will save you a lot of time and frustration when you start studying as you will then be able to concentrate on the actual subject matter itself without the need to refer back to what you are supposed to be doing with each part.

At the outset you are assumed to have no prior knowledge or experience of the subject and can expect to be taken logically, step by step from start to finish of the learning programme. To help you take on new ideas and information, and to help you remember and apply them, you will come across many different and challenging self check tasks, activities, quizzes and questions which you should approach seriously and enthusiastically. These features are designed not only to make your learning easier and more interesting but to help you to apply what you are studying to your own work situation in a practical and down-to-earth way.

To help to scan the workbook and cassette properly, and to understand what you find, here is a summary of the main features:

The workbook

If you want:	Refer to:
To see which other Super Series 2 units can also help you with this topic	The Study links
An overview of every part of the workbook and how the book and audio cassette link together	The Unit map
A list of the main knowledge and skill outcomes you will gain from the unit	The Unit objectives
To check on your understanding of the subject and your progress as you work thorough each section	The Activities and Self checks
To test how much you have understood and learned of the whole unit when your studies are complete	The Quick quiz and Action checks
An assessment by a third party for work done and time spent on this unit for purposes of recognition, award or certification	The Unit assessment The Work-based assignment
To put some of the things learned from the unit into practice in your own work situation	The Action plan (where present)

If you want:	Refer to:
To start your study of the unit	The Introduction: Side one
To check your knowledge of the complete unit	The Quick quiz: Side one
To check your ability to apply what you have learned to 'real life' by listening to some situations and deciding what you should do or say	The Action checks: Side two

Managing your learning programme

When you feel you know your way around the material, and in particular appreciate the progress checking and assessment features, the next stage is to put together your own personal study plan and decide how best to study.

These two things are just as important as checking out the material; they are also useful time savers and give you the satisfaction of feeling organized and knowing exactly where you are going and what you are trying to achieve.

You have already chosen your subject (this unit) so you should now decide when you need to finish the unit and how much time you must spend to make sure you reach your target.

To help you to answer these questions, you should know that each workbook and audio cassette will probably take about *eight* to *ten* hours to complete; the variation in time allows for different reading, writing and study speeds and the length and complexity of any one subject.

Don't be concerned if it takes you longer than these average times, especially on your first unit, and always keep in mind that the objective of your training is understanding and applying the learning, not competing in a race.

Experience has shown that each unit is best completed over a two-week period with about *three* to *four* study hours spent on it in each week, and about *one* to *two* hours at each sitting. These times are about right for tackling a new subject and still keeping work and other commitments sensibly in balance.

Using these time guides you should set, and try to keep to, specific times, days, and dates for your study. You should write down what you have decided and keep it visible as a reminder. If you are studying more than one unit, probably as part of a larger training programme, then the compilation of a full, dated plan or schedule becomes even more important and might have to tie in with dates and times set by others, such as a tutor.

The next step is to decide where to study. If you are doing this training in conjunction with your company or organization this might be decided for you as most have quiet areas, training rooms, learning centres, etc., which you will be encouraged to use. If you are working at home, set aside a quiet corner where books and papers can be left and kept together with a comfortable chair and a simple writing surface. You will also need a note pad and access to cassette playing equipment.

When you are finally ready to start studying, presuming that you are feeling confident and organized after your preparations, you should follow the instructions given in the Unit Map and the Unit Objectives pages. These tell you to play the first part of Side one of the audio cassette, a couple of times is a good idea, then follow the cues back to the workbook.

You should then work through each workbook section doing all that is asked of you until you reach the final assessments. Don't forget to keep your eye on the Unit Map as you progress and try to finish each session at a sensible point in the unit, ideally at the end of a complete section or part. You should always start your next session by looking back, for at least ten to fifteen minutes, at the work you did in the previous session.

You are encouraged to retain any reports, work-based assignments or other material produced in conjunction with your work through this unit in case you wish to present these later as evidence for a competency award or accreditation of prior learning.

Help, guidance and tutorial support

The workbook and audio cassette have been designed to be as self-contained as possible, acting as your guide and tutor throughout your studies. However, there are bound to be times when you might not quite understand what the author is saying, or perhaps you don't agree with a certain point. Whatever the reason, we all need help and support from time to time and Open Learners are no exception.

Help during Open Learning study can come in many forms, providing you are prepared to seek it out and use it:

- first of all you could help yourself. Perhaps you are giving up too easily. Go back over it and try again;

- or you could ask your family or friends. Even if they don't understand the subject, the act of discussing it sometimes clarifies things in your own mind;

- then there is your company trainer or superior. If you are training as part of a company scheme, and during work time, then help and support will probably have been arranged for you already. Help and advice under these circumstances are important, especially as they can help you interpret your studies through actual and relevant company examples;

- if you are pursuing this training on your own, you could enlist expert help from a local Open Learning centre or agency. Such organizations exist in considerable numbers throughout the UK, often linked to colleges and other training establishments. The National Examining Board for Supervisory Management (NEBSM or NEBS Management), has several hundred such centres and can provide not only help and support but full assessment and accreditation facilities if you want to pursue a qualification as part of your chosen programme.

The NEBSM Super Series second edition is a selection of workbook and audio cassette packages covering a wide range of supervisory and first line management topics.

Although the individual books and cassettes are completely self-contained and cover single subject areas, each belongs to one of the four modular groups shown. These groups can help you build up your personal development programme as you can easily see which subjects are related. The groups are also important if you undertake any NEBSM national award programme.

Managing Human Resources	HR1	Supervising at Work	HR10	Managing Time
	HR2	Supervising with Authority	HR11	Hiring People
	HR3	Team Leading	HR12	Interviewing
	HR4	Delegation	HR13	Training Plans
	HR5	Workteams	HR14	Training Sessions
	HR6	Motivating People	HR15	Industrial Relations
	HR7	Leading Change	HR16	Employment and the Law
	HR8	Personnel in Action	HR17	Equality at Work
	HR9	Performance Appraisal		
Managing Information	IN1	Communicating	IN7	Using Statistics
	IN2	Speaking Skills	IN8	Presenting Figures
	IN3	Orders and Instructions	IN9	Introduction to Information Technology
	IN4	Meetings		
	IN5	Writing Skills	IN10	Computers and Communication Systems
	IN6	Project Preparation		
Managing Financial Resources	FR1	Accounting for Money	FR4	Pay Systems
	FR2	Control via Budgets	FR5	Security
	FR3	Controlling Costs		
Managing Products and Services	PS1	Controlling Work	PS7	Solving Problems
	PS2	Health and Safety	PS8	Productivity
	PS3	Accident Prevention	PS9	Stock Control Systems
	PS4	Ensuring Quality	PS10	Stores Control
	PS5	Quality Techniques	PS11	Efficiency in the Office
	PS6	Taking Decisions	PS12	Marketing

While the contents have been thoroughly updated, many Super Series 2 titles remain the same as, or very similar to the first edition units. Where, through merger, rewrite or deletion title changes have also been made, this summary should help you. If you are in any doubt please contact Pergamon Open Learning direct.

First Edition	**Second Edition**
Merged titles	
105 Organization Systems and 106 Supervising in the System	HR1 Supervising at Work
100 Needs and Rewards and 101 Enriching Work	HR6 Motivating People
502 Discipline and the Law and 508 Supervising and the Law	HR16 Employment and the Law
204 Easy Statistics and 213 Descriptive Statistics	IN7 Using Statistics
200 Looking at Figures and 202 Using Graphs	IN8 Presenting Figures
210 Computers and 303 Communication Systems	IN10 Computers and Communication Systems
402 Cost Reduction and 405 Cost Centres	FR3 Controlling Costs
203 Method Study and 208 Value Analysis	PS8 Productivity
Major title changes	
209 Quality Circles	PS4 Ensuring Quality
205 Quality Control	PS5 Quality Techniques
Deleted titles	
406 National Economy/410 Single European Market	

The NEBSM Super Series 2 Open Learning material is published by Pergamon Open Learning in conjunction with NEBS Management.

NEBS Management is the largest provider of management education, training courses and qualifications in the United Kingdom, operating through over 600 Centres. Many of these Centres offer Open Learning and can provide help to individual students.

Many thousands of students follow the Open Learning route with great success and gain NEBSM or other qualifications.

NEBSM offers qualifications and awards at three levels:

- the NEBSM Introductory Award in Supervisory Management;
- the NEBSM Certificate in Supervisory Management;
- the NEBSM Diploma in Supervisory Management.

The NEBSM Super Series 2 Open Learning material is designed for use at Introductory and Certificate levels.

The **Introductory Award** requires a minimum of 30 hours of study and provides a grounding in the theory and practice of supervisory management. An agreed programme of five NEBSM Super Series 2 units plus a one-day workshop satisfactorily completed can lead to this Award. Pre-approved topic combinations exist for general, industrial and commercial needs. Completed Super Series 2 units can count towards the full NEBSM Certificate.

The **Certificate in Supervisory Management** requires study of up to 25 NEBSM Super Series 2 units and participation in group activity or workshops. The assessment system includes work-based assignments, a case study, a project and an oral interview. The certificate is divided into four modules and each may be completed separately. A **Module Award** can be made on successful completion of each module, and when the full assessments are satisfactorily completed the Certificate is awarded. Students will need to register with a NEBSM Centre in order to enter for an award – NEBSM can advise you.

Students wishing to gain recognition of competence as defined by the Management Charter Initiative (MCI) or National Vocational Qualification (NVQ) lead bodies, will find that Open Learning material provides the necessary knowledge and skills required for this purpose.

Progression

Many successful NEBSM students use their qualifications as stepping stones to other awards, both educational and professional. Recognition is given by a number of bodies for this purpose. Further details about this and other NEBSM matters can be obtained from:

NEBSM Information Officer
The National Examining Board for Supervisory Management
76 Portland Place
London W1N 4AA

Competence-based programmes

Super Series 2 units can be used to provide the necessary underpinning knowledge, skills and understanding that are required to prepare yourself for competence-based assessment.

Working through Super Series 2 units cannot, by itself, provide you with everything you need to enter or be entered for competence assessment. This must come from a combination of skill, experience and knowledge gained both on and off the job. If you wish to pursue an Open Learning route to a competence-based award you are advised to check with NEBSM as to when and where this type of assessment will be available through them, and with MCI at the address below, as to the actual competency units that need to be assessed as these are subject to change.

Management Charter Initiative
c/o Shell UK Ltd
Shell-mex House
Strand
London
WC2R 0DX

You will also find many of the 44 Super Series 2 units of use in learning programmes for other National Vocational Qualifications (NVQs) which include elements of supervisory management. Please check with the relevant NVQ lead body for information on units of competence and underlying knowledge, skills and understanding.

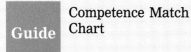

Guide | Competence Match Chart

The Competence Match Chart illustrates which Super Series 2 units provide background vital to the current Management Charter Initiative (MCI) Supervisory sub-set Units of Competence.

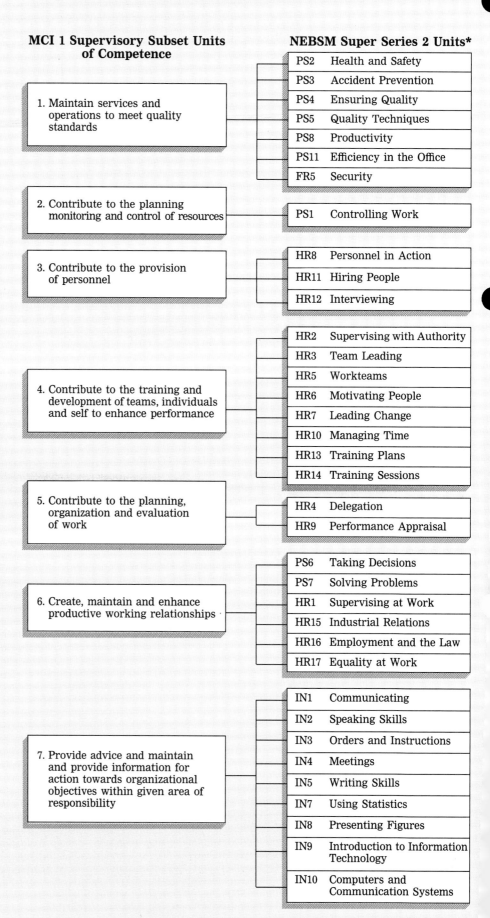

MCI 1 Supervisory Subset Units of Competence

1. Maintain services and operations to meet quality standards

2. Contribute to the planning monitoring and control of resources

3. Contribute to the provision of personnel

4. Contribute to the training and development of teams, individuals and self to enhance performance

5. Contribute to the planning, organization and evaluation of work

6. Create, maintain and enhance productive working relationships

7. Provide advice and maintain and provide information for action towards organizational objectives within given area of responsibility

NEBSM Super Series 2 Units*

PS2	Health and Safety
PS3	Accident Prevention
PS4	Ensuring Quality
PS5	Quality Techniques
PS8	Productivity
PS11	Efficiency in the Office
FR5	Security

PS1	Controlling Work

HR8	Personnel in Action
HR11	Hiring People
HR12	Interviewing

HR2	Supervising with Authority
HR3	Team Leading
HR5	Workteams
HR6	Motivating People
HR7	Leading Change
HR10	Managing Time
HR13	Training Plans
HR14	Training Sessions

HR4	Delegation
HR9	Performance Appraisal

PS6	Taking Decisions
PS7	Solving Problems
HR1	Supervising at Work
HR15	Industrial Relations
HR16	Employment and the Law
HR17	Equality at Work

IN1	Communicating
IN2	Speaking Skills
IN3	Orders and Instructions
IN4	Meetings
IN5	Writing Skills
IN7	Using Statistics
IN8	Presenting Figures
IN9	Introduction to Information Technology
IN10	Computers and Communication Systems

Please note that the Super Series 2 contains eight additional units relevant to supervisory management (see page ix).

Unit Completion Certificate

Completion of this Certificate by an authorized and qualified person indicates that you have worked through all parts of this unit and completed all assessments. If you are studying this unit as part of a certificated programme, or think you may wish to in future, then completion of this Certificate is particularly important as it may be used for exemptions, credit accumulation or Accreditation of Prior Learning (APL). Full details can be obtained from NEBSM.

NEBSM
SUPER SERIES
Second Edition

PS12

Marketing

. . . .

has satisfactorily completed this unit.

Name of Signatory. . . . .

Position. . . . .

Signature. . . . .

Date . . . .

Official Stamp

Keep in touch

Pergamon Open Learning and NEBS Management are always happy to hear of your experiences of using the Super Series to help improve supervisory and managerial effectiveness. This will assist us with continuous product improvement, and novel approaches and success stories may be included in promotional information to illustrate to others what can be done.

1   NEBSM Super Series 2 study links

Here are the Super Series 2 units which link to *Marketing*. You may find this useful when you are putting together your study programme but you should bear in mind that:

- each Super Series 2 unit stands alone and does not depend upon being used in conjunction with any other unit;

- Super Series 2 units can be used in any order which suits your learning needs.

CONTROLLING WORK
This unit deals with techniques to help you plan, monitor and control work.

LEADING CHANGE
To remain competitive, organizations need to be continually prepared to change to meet the needs of customers.

PRESENTING FIGURES
Organizing and displaying information as tables, charts, graphs and diagrams – all useful marketing aids.

MARKETING
This unit will help you to take a marketing approach to identification of your customers and your customers' needs.

ENSURING QUALITY
Quality is as important to effective marketing as it is to any other function.

COMMUNICATING
Understanding how good communications can help in effective marketing is a useful skill.

CONTROLLING COSTS
How to achieve target costs and prevent costs rising - an essential part of remaining competitively in the market.

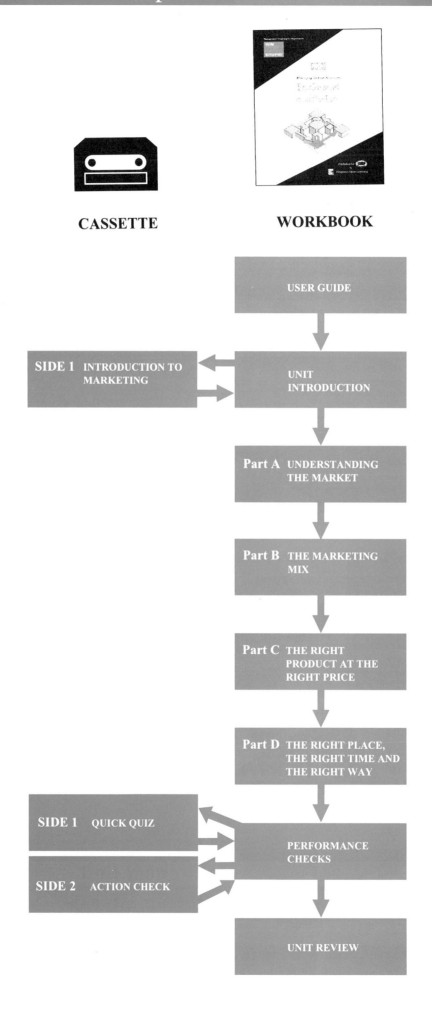

CASSETTE   WORKBOOK

USER GUIDE

SIDE 1   INTRODUCTION TO
          MARKETING

UNIT
INTRODUCTION

Part A   UNDERSTANDING
          THE MARKET

Part B   THE MARKETING
          MIX

Part C   THE RIGHT
          PRODUCT AT THE
          RIGHT PRICE

Part D   THE RIGHT PLACE,
          THE RIGHT TIME AND
          THE RIGHT WAY

SIDE 1   QUICK QUIZ

SIDE 2   ACTION CHECK

PERFORMANCE
CHECKS

UNIT REVIEW

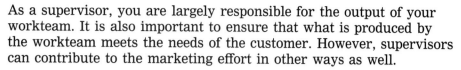

Intro

As a supervisor, you are largely responsible for the output of your workteam. It is also important to ensure that what is produced by the workteam meets the needs of the customer. However, supervisors can contribute to the marketing effort in other ways as well.

This unit sets out to make the point that everyone in an organization is involved in the marketing process. The supervisor has the ideal opportunity to ensure that all the members of the workteam have an awareness of marketing.

Before you start work on the unit, listen carefully to Side one of the audio cassette, which sets the scene for your examination of *Marketing*.

In this unit we will:

● take a close look at what it means to operate inside the market, and see what is meant by the marketing approach;

● spell out in detail what goes into the marketing mix;

● explain the many ways in which a supervisor's work can help or hinder the marketing approach.

Objectives

When you have worked through this unit, you will be ***better able to***:

● understand what is meant by the market and the marketing approach, and how important they are in the modern world;

● understand the marketing mix, and how an organization's resources are used to satisfy customers' needs;

● adopt the marketing approach and apply it to your everyday activities.

UNDERSTANDING THE MARKET

1 Introduction

Over the last 100 years whole industries have been swept away, and entirely new ones have come from nowhere. Caring for horses used to be one of the biggest service industries, with numerous stables in every town. Hundreds of thousands of people earned their living by manufacturing pieces of harness and equipment for horse-drawn vehicles. On a bigger scale, shipbuilding firms were thriving at ports everywhere in Britain.

Today these major industries have almost vanished.

On the other hand, even in 1970 there was virtually no computer industry, no satellite communications, and no video business.

Why have the old industries withered away? They possessed tremendous skills and expertise, and they had dedicated workers. The product they produced was often first-rate.

The problem was simply *that their customers didn't want those products any more* – there were other products on offer that they preferred.

This is a most important lesson. All of us tend to become justifiably proud of our skills and expertise at our jobs, and even of the equipment that we use. We tend to focus on the product, and forget the customer. But in the end, we have to have to recognize that making a top-quality stage coach when the customer wants an economical two-tonne van is the road to ruin.

This unit is about changing focus, about thinking about the market and the customer first, and the product itself second. This may sound topsy turvey, but in today's world, meeting the customers' needs is what counts, and the product itself is just one part of the approach to doing so.

2 The market, competition and business

**2.1
What is
'the market'?**

You will often hear people talk about 'the market', or read about it in the newspapers, but the word *market* is used in many different contexts. For example:

- the Stock Market;
- the cattle market;
- the Common Market;
- the export market;
- the money market;
- the commodities market.

In all these examples a 'market' is a place where things are brought to be bought and sold, but what do all these markets have in common?

Activity 1

■ Time guide 8 minutes

Think about your local open-air market – perhaps a fruit and vegetable market. Describe in about 50 words what goes on there.

_____

_____

_____

_____

_____

_____

_____

I would describe it like this:

'A number of different traders bring their goods and set them out on stalls. Then lots of potential customers come along and decide what they will buy, and from which trader they will buy it. The traders each try to sell their goods by offering the customer sharper pricing, or more attractive displays, or by shouting louder.'

There are two things to notice about this description:

the market forces the trader to face competition;

the market presents the customer with choice.

However, when we talk about 'the Market' in a *general* sense, we are referring to a whole world system which is conducted on this basis.

The Market is simply the way in which the supply of goods and services, both nationally and internationally, is organized, though 'organized' is perhaps the wrong word to use about it. The Market is not organized in the way that a factory or an office is. *It is the net product of limitless numbers of buyers meeting limitless numbers of sellers, and hence of millions and millions of individual decisions.* The Market is very difficult to predict, and it is constantly changing. It is almost impossible to control, except in very limited and specialized areas where there are few sellers and buyers.

But the Market, with brutal clarity, tells each seller whether or not his product will succeed. This is the so-called 'law of supply and demand', and in this respect, the market is a very effective mechanism for deciding, on a global scale, what goods and services will be produced and how much they can sell for.

However, it is not the only mechanism for doing this. The 'Soviet Bloc' countries did not operate a market system. Instead, central planning authorities decided what would be produced, where, when, and in what quantities. This system did have some advantages, but the majority of the Soviet Bloc's people chose the market system, once they got the chance to do so.

We all operate inside the Market, and every organization, in some sense, lays its wares out on a stall in front of the buying public. For commercial organizations, success in the market place is crucial because it brings in the cash needed for survival.

The 'market approach' increasingly applies to non-commercial organizations too – from hospitals, schools and government departments right down to voluntary bodies, Local Authority Social Services and even prisons.

All of them need to market themselves: they need funds, equipment, staff, 'clients', volunteer workers, donations and so on. And just like industry and commerce, they have to compete to get them.

**2.2
The product**

People who work in manufacturing industry will naturally think of the things which they make as 'products'. These may be pipes or pickles, tanks or tintacks, but they are something physical that they can point to and say: "That's our product'.

Retailers can also point to a series of products, but many of us work in organizations whose product is something less material: banks and building societies for instance.

Activity 2

■ Time guide 3 minutes

Try to list *five* 'products' offered by one or two of the big high-street banks.

_____

_____

_____

_____

_____

Financial institutions like these have many products (they do actually refer to them as 'products'). They include current accounts, deposit accounts, TESSAs, mortgages, loans, foreign exchange, bill payment services, insurance, savings plans, pensions schemes and so on.

These are what the banks try to sell in their part of the market place.

Throughout this unit, I will be using the word 'product' to refer to whatever an organization has to offer in its market place, whether that is goods, services, or something else.

Something else? 'Marketing' and 'products' are words we naturally associate with profit-making commercial organizations. But increasingly, non-commercial organizations are having to think in the same way. Hospitals' product is health, schools deal in education. And even charities have products to market – even when that product is something like 'feeding the hungry' or 'the satisfaction of giving to charity'.

**2.3
Competition**

Imagine a world where there was only one source of a particular important product – say smoke detectors. This situation is known as a monopoly.

Everyone who wanted a smoke detector badly enough would have to go to that one supplier. The supplier wouldn't need to bother with appearances: the business could be run from a dirty old shed. Convenience wouldn't matter much either: the firm could be located in Greenland. Publicity could be ignored: the customers would tell each other where to find it. And service, packaging, quality and price would be of no importance.

Now, there are a lot of organizations which would secretly like to operate that way, but in practice monopolies are rather rare. In every area of activity which is capable of being profitable, there is always competition.

Activity 3

▇ Time guide 5 minutes

Here are three different enterprises. For each one, say who its competitors might be, and why.

The Tower of London

_____

_____

_____

Your local travel agent

_____

_____

_____

British Steel

_____

_____

_____

The easiest of these to answer is the third one. British Steel obviously competes with steel-makers. There are a few independent steel makers in Britain, but most of the competition comes from big firms based in other countries. So British Steel competes in an international market for steel.

The first example, a famous tourist attraction, may have given you pause for thought. But tourist attractions do have to compete, even if many visitors want specifically to visit this particular place. In the long run, if the Tower of London were to become too expensive, or too shoddy, or if the staff were too unhelpful, it would lose out to other tourist attractions. So we are correct in saying that the Tower of London is in competition with all the other tourist sites in London.

To some extent it also competes with other cities – Cambridge, Edinburgh, Paris or Rome – because it is part of London's general 'competitive pitch' for the international tourist market.

And we can go a step further: the Tower also competes *with other things that people could be spending their time and money doing*, from watching TV to taking a river trip or going to the races.

The same applies to the local travel agent. Obviously, each travel agent has to compete with its business rivals, but it also has to compete with other products that families might spend their money on. A sum of £700 spent on a holiday could have been spent on new carpets, a hi-fi, or dozens of other things.

So my point here is two-fold:

every organized enterprise faces competition;

competition does not necessarily come just from the
obvious business rivals.

Activity 4

■ Time guide 3 minutes

Now think about your own organization (or if you are not working at present, one that you know well).

■ What are its main products?

_____

_____

_____

■ Who are its main competitors?

_____

_____

_____

The point of that question was to remind you:

● that your organization does have competitors;

● that whatever part of the organization you work in, competing with them successfully is of vital importance to your personal future.

No-one can afford to ignore the market, and everyone is forced to compete. Competition demands hard work, clear vision, skills and resources. The penalties of failure are decline, job losses, and eventually bankruptcy or take-over.

The rewards of success are growth, expansion and opportunity. So performance in the market is a key issue for every employee in your organization.

3	Product life-cycles

The market is all about the buying and selling of products – goods, services or whatever. But the market has a ruthless way with products, and even the most successful products do not go on for ever. The world of the market is constantly changing, and unless the products also change, they will be left behind and forgotten.

Organizations which wish to live longer than any of the particular products they offer, are obliged to do two things:

> modify existing products to ensure that they meet the requirements of today's market;

> introduce new products that will meet the needs of tomorrow's market.

In the business world this has produced some remarkable changes.

One of the most spectacular is the firm that makes Rose's Lime Juice. In the nineteenth century, it was a shipping company, and it supplied its sailors with lime juice to prevent scurvy. As the markets changed, the firm abandoned the shipping operation and concentrated on the lime-juice business!

Activity 5

■ Time guide 3 minutes

What new products has the organization you work for introduced in the last three years?

_____

_____

_____

_____

No doubt your existing products were also modified in various ways. The big car manufacturers are a good example of this. Marques like the Ford Fiesta, the Austin Metro and the Renault 5 have been around for many years, but every two or three years, the manufacturers carry out a significant upgrade, and re-launch improved models on the market.

In the commercial world, the introduction of new products is most important for long-term success.

Successful commercial products typically pass through a four-stage life-cycle.

● Stage 1
Research, development, tooling and planning, production, promotion, advertising, and launch on the market.

● Stage 2
Rapid sales growth, competitive advantage and high profits.

● Stage 3
Sales still good, but competition increasing and profitability declining (the market is 'mature').

● Stage 4
Product outdated, fierce competition, price falling, sales and profits in decline (the market is 'saturated').

Of course, some products live longer than others, while many never get beyond Stage 2.

In graph form, the product life-cycle looks like this:

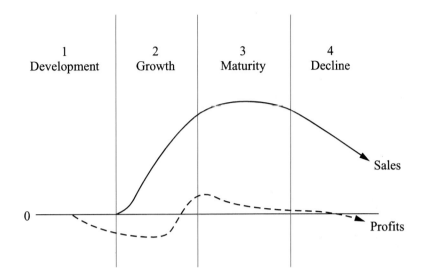

Clearly, before the graph starts dropping in Stage 3, new products must come into the picture, so that sales overall are kept stable.

Because predicting the way the market will move in future is so difficult, most new products do not do well. The proportion that succeed in a big way is tiny (perhaps only one per cent). So most businesses try to keep up a steady flow of product innovation so that the chances of at least one product succeeding are reasonably high.

But even though it is difficult, the better we can predict the market, the less the risk of failure. That is an essential part of the marketing approach.

4   The marketing approach

**4.1
A definition**

Marketing is often taken to mean promotion and selling – advertising, for example. But the marketing approach broadens this definition considerably.

Activity 6

◾ Time guide 4 minutes

How would you define 'marketing'?

_____

_____

_____

Actually there are several widely accepted definitions, all of which vary slightly. For example, we could say:

'Marketing is whatever needs to be done to ensure success in the market place',

but my preference is for:

'Marketing is the process of identifying and satisfying the needs of the customer.'

We can 'unpack' this definition by saying that marketing consists of the following basic processes.

- **Market research**:

  – finding out who the customers are;
  – finding out what they need;
  – finding out who else is trying to meet the need.

- **Product development**:

  – developing a product that meets the need;
  – making stocks available at the right place, at the right time and in the right way.

- **Promotion and selling**:

  – informing the customer about the product;
  – encouraging them to choose it.

Another, simpler way to put this is to say that marketing is about providing:

- the right product;

- at the right price;

- at the right place;

- at the right time;

- in the right way.

Whichever way we look at it, the marketing approach is about 'getting it right'.

We could even call this a **total marketing approach**, because absolutely every aspect of the business is relevant to success or failure in the market. Organizations that follow the marketing approach understand that everything they do has to be geared to market success.

Extension 1 If you would like to find out more about how the marketing approach works, and what happens to organizations which do not adopt it, I suggest you look at R. G. I. Maxwell's book, *Marketing*, which is listed as one of our extensions.

In this approach, customers' needs are more important than superb production skills or time-honoured systems and procedures. The needs of the market **always come first**!

**4.2
Market research**

Market research, meaning the process of increasing our knowledge of the market – is a vitally important part of getting it right. But what knowledge do we need?

Activity 7

■ Time guide 3 minutes

Ted and Lucy came into some money, and decided to give up their jobs and start a business making and selling radio-controlled models.

What would you say were the *three* most important aspects of the market that they would need to research before making the decision to begin?

_____

_____

_____

It is most important to find out about the total size and money value of the market, and the nature and strength of the competition as they are at present:

■ how many people in the area are interested in these products;

■ how much they are likely to spend on them;

■ who the competitors are, what they do, and where they are located.

Extension 2 If you would like to go into the subject of market research in more depth, and learn about some of the techniques involved, I suggest you look at *Do Your Own Market Research*, by P. N. Hague and P. Jackson.

Activity 8

■ Time guide 3 minutes

It is difficult for market research to predict the future, but try to suggest *three* things that researchers could investigate to help Ted and Lucy predict the future potential of the market for radio-controlled models:

_____

_____

_____

This activity may have been difficult for you if you have no previous knowledge of marketing, but since radio-controlled models are expensive toys, I think I would want to know about potential customers as well as actual ones:

■ what sort of people they are likely to be;

■ how many such people there are;

■ whether their numbers are likely to increase or decrease;

■ what might be done to turn these potential customers into actual customers.

13

Increasingly, consumer market research is looking at:

- lifestyles and attitudes rather than simply income and spending patterns;

- general economic changes that will influence spending patterns over a period of years.

So we can sum up the tasks of market research like this:

> research needs to find out the present state of the market and how it is likely to change in the future.

This applies to every kind of organization which operates in a market, whether its products are goods or services, whether it is large or small, and whether its market is local, national, or international.

And all in all, market research is very big business – but it does not take decisions.

That can be done only by managers, using the research figures, and perhaps helped by marketing specialists. So obviously, the marketing approach demands a great deal of hard-headed but creative thought and planning, right from the very beginning.

**4.3
New product
development**

Activity 9

■ Time guide 3 minutes

Every organization has to decide what attitude it will take towards its product and its customers. Which of these three attitudes is closest to that of your own organization?

■ Build a better mousetrap and the world will beat a path to your door. ☐

■ Build a worse mousetrap, and spend a lot of money on advertising, and the world will beat a path to your door. ☐

■ Find out what sort of a mousetrap the customer wants, then produce it and tell them. ☐

The people who design and develop a new product are usually experts on their subject.

Whether it is an insurance firm planning a new product such as a policy for people buying holiday homes abroad, or an electronics company designing a new type of car alarm, highly experienced and expert people will be involved.

However, experience suggests that, left to themselves, the experts will probably come up with a product which does its job brilliantly but is too complex and expensive for the market. It will be 'over-engineered', in design terms. That is the 'Build a better mousetrap' attitude: a product-led operation.

Product-led organizations can easily find themselves deeply disappointed when their superb product fails to sell, because it was what they wanted, but not what the market wanted.

On the other hand, those organizations which don't care about product quality at all, but expect the marketing people to lie their way to success, are also doomed to disappointment: a worse mousetrap will soon be seen for what it is.

The third attitude is more likely to be successful. The needs of the market over-ride the needs of the product and its designers, so 'market-led' organizations:

- first study their market;

- then give the development and production people a specification designed to meet the market's needs;

- then get the product produced;

- then market it in a positive and effective way.

4.4
Product distribution

One of the worst disasters that can happen in marketing is for the customers to be ready and eager to buy a new product, only to find that it isn't available.

Activity 10

■ Time guide 3 minutes

A new range of cook–chill meals was due to hit the shops on 1 June. The advertising campaign was booked and all the promotional activities were ready to go.

Suggest *three* things that could happen to prevent the product being ready on time:

_____

_____

_____

All sorts of things could happen, including:

- delays in the production process;

- the discovery of last-minute quality problems;

- a fire in the warehouse;

- mistakes over physical distribution arrangements;

- packaging faults;

- disputes with the retailers or suppliers.

What this catalogue of possible disasters shows is that many people, working in many different parts of an organization, all have an important role to play in getting the product onto the market.

> The success of a promotional campaign depends on everything else being ready too.

4.5
Promotion

Promotion covers all the information and 'selling' activities that the marketing and advertising people undertake. These are specialized activities which are beyond the scope of this unit, but that is not to underestimate their importance.

It can be the right product, at the right time, and at the right price for the market, but there are lots of other products out there, all jostling for the customer's attention, and all with skilful and determined people promoting them.

Unless the product achieves the right impact in that crowded market, it will sink without trace.

■ Time guide 8 minutes

Fill in the blanks so that these statements make sense.

1. The market forces traders to face _____ and presents customers with _____.

2. The market is the net result of millions and millions of individual _____.

3. We refer to whatever an organization offers to the market as the _____.

4. Even the most successful product has a limited _____ – _____.

5. Market research is mainly concerned with finding out about the _____ market.

6. It is much more difficult for market research to _____ the _____ even though it is vitally important to try to do so.

7. It is rather rare for a particular organization to have a _____ in the market.

8. The marketing approach can be seen as providing:

   (a) the right _____;

   (b) at the right _____;

   (c) at the right _____;

   (d) at the right _____;

   (e) in the right _____.

Response check 1

1. The market forces traders to face COMPETITION and presents customers with CHOICE.

2. The market is the net result of millions and millions of individual DECISIONS.

3. We refer to whatever an organization offers to the market as the PRODUCT.

4. Even the most successful product has a limited LIFE-CYCLE (or LIFE-TIME).

5. Market research is mainly concerned with finding out about the EXISTING market.

6. It is much more difficult for market research to PREDICT the future, even though it is vitally important to try to do so.

7. It is rather rare for a particular organization to have a MONOPOLY in the market.

8. The marketing approach can be seen as providing:

   (a) the right PRODUCT;

   (b) at the right PRICE;

   (c) at the right TIME;

   (d) at the right PLACE;

   (e) in the right WAY.

- The market is a system under which large numbers of traders offer goods or services for sale and large numbers of customers choose which to buy. The market's decisions are the net product of millions of individual decisions.

- Every organized enterprise faces competition; monopolies are rare.

- Competition does not necessarily come from the obvious business rivals.

- The goods, services or activities that an organization markets are known in general as its 'products'.

- All products have a limited life-cycle. Commercial organizations need to keep developing new products, to ensure their long-term survival.

- Marketing can be defined as 'The process of identifying and satisfying the needs of the customer'. It can also be seen as providing:

  - the right product;

  - at the right price;

  - at the right time;

  - at the right place;

  - in the right way.

- Every aspect of an organization is relevant to its success or failure in the market place.

- Market research looks mainly at the existing market:

  - the number and location of the customers;

  - how much they have to spend;

  - who the competitors are.

- Market research also tries to predict how the market will be in the future; but this is difficult.

- 'Product-led' organizations start with their products, and then look for ways of marketing them.

- 'Market-led' organizations:

  - first study their market;

  - then specify a product that will meet the market's needs;

  - then produce the product;

  - then promote it effectively.

- The most successful organizations are market-led and adopt a 'total marketing approach'.

17

THE MARKETING MIX

1   Introduction

'The Marketing Mix' is a jargon term, but the idea behind it is very significant, because every product on the market is different, even if the differences only seem small.

Take petrol, for example.

All four-star unleaded petrol is the same, regardless of whether it is sold by Shell, Texaco, BP or anyone else. Even the price does not vary greatly between different petrol retailers. However, every petrol company presents its petrol to the public in a slightly different way. Some have extensive forecourt shops and other facilities, others simply have a kiosk. Some offer stamps, gifts and other promotional inducements; others don't. Some concentrate on big trunk-road sites; others go for smaller urban locations. Some put their staff in uniform, others don't. And overall, the style, décor, layout and advertising of the different companies are distinctly different.

All the details which distinguish an Elf station from a Q8 station, and from all the others, play a part in building up the overall 'package' that the company offers to its customers. Individually, the impact of the details may be quite small, but together they make up a distinctive marketing mix. (And actually, the petrol is the least important part of the marketing mix for petrol companies: their marketing people regard **the petrol station** as the product, not the fuel sold there.)

These differences are crucial in enabling the rivals to compete. They cannot truthfully say things like 'Buy Octopus petrol because it makes your car go faster', but they can say 'Buy Octopus petrol because our service is better', or 'because our stations are cleaner and more modern', or 'because we share your particular lifestyle'. Advertising people can come up with plenty of variations on that theme!

2   The elements of the marketing mix

The marketing mix is the sum total of all the elements that go to make up the 'offer' that an organization makes to its market. Broadly, the elements are those which we looked at briefly under 'the marketing approach' in Part A:

- the right product;
- at the right price;
- at the right place;
- at the right time;
- in the right way.

An organization that gets all those elements right may not sweep the market, but it will be able to compete; one that does not won't even be in the running.

**2.1
Competing for
customers**

Example 1: building
societies

There are a lot of different building societies, and almost every town
centre contains several branches. They all sell a similar range of
deposit accounts, current accounts, loans and mortgages, and yet
they have to compete.

Activity 11

■ Time guide 5 minutes

Suppose you moved to a new town, and decided to start up a deposit account with a
building society. You have no particular preference, but you will need to visit the branch
perhaps three or four times a month. There are six different building societies in town from
which you could choose.

List *ten* factors that might influence your choice.

_____

_____

_____

_____

_____

_____

_____

_____

_____

_____

Price (meaning the rate of interest paid and charged) will obviously
be a factor; most investors would try to find the best rate of interest
in town.

But this would have to be weighed against other factors, such as
convenience. If you have to visit the branch several times a month,
you would probably prefer it to be located:

■ in an easily accessible area;

■ close to car parking facilities;

■ close to the other facilities that you might need (such as shops,
post office, library etc.).

Other convenience factors like *opening hours* might also count. Will
the branch be open when you need it? Are enough staff on duty
during busy times, so that you can avoid long waits? Do they offer
other products that you might be interested in?

Then there is the *human factor* – the staff. Are they friendly,
helpful, smart? Do they seem to have enough knowledge and
expertise to talk sensibly about your needs?

And what about the general *style and décor* of the premises? Smart,
scruffy, modern, old-fashioned, spacious, colourful, drab, warm,
draughty, stuffy, noisy – these are all matters that have an impact on
customers. Is the exterior clean? Is the window display neat and
attractive?

Finally, there is the *image* of the society created by its advertising. The large societies spend large sums of money on informing the public about the products they offer, but also on building a particular image, which may be caring, efficient, business like, hi-tech, relaxed-and-friendly, and so on. Like the décor and window displays of their local branches, these are not necessarily factors of which we are conscious when we make buying decisions, but subconsciously they affect us.

There is many a customer who can say 'No, I don't fancy that place', without being able to say exactly why. In reality, the customer's attitude is formed by the sum total of all the elements in the marketing mix, some of which are not immediately obvious, such as 'style'.

Example 2:
a manufacturing
company

CDT Sensors Ltd. make digital analysers – specialized machines for testing the circuitry of micro-electronic equipment. They sell a small range of products and accessories to companies which make and repair such equipment. Their market is this narrow slice of a few thousand business users. They do not sell to the general public at all.

The company advertises in trade magazines, exhibits at trade shows and has four sales representatives who constantly travel the country.

Activity 12

■ Time guide 4 minutes

List *six* things that would probably be important elements in the marketing mix of a firm like CDT Sensors Ltd.

_____

_____

_____

_____

_____

_____

In this case we already know about two factors that will weigh heavily:

■ the products themselves with all their features and benefits;

■ the advertising, promotional and selling activities.

Other important elements in the mix will include:

■ price, including discount structure;

■ availability of stocks and delivery lead times;

■ service and technical back-up.

There might even be special factors such as the amount of training offered to customers in how to operate the machines. And of course, the details of every aspect of the operation will count, perhaps subconsciously: the reps, their cars, the quality of the exhibition panels and descriptive literature offered, and so on.

The mixture of all these different elements is what CDT Sensors Ltd set out on their 'market stall' to try and win customers; and their particular mixture needs to be different in some way to what their competitors are offering, in order to give them a competitive edge.

We can sum up what these two examples show us by saying that:

- everything that has an effect on the customer is part of the marketing mix, and this is true whether those concerned are aware of it or not;

- some factors weigh more heavily than others;

- customers make conscious decisions about some factors, but others have a sub-conscious effect.

In general, the most important elements of the marketing mix are:

- the product itself;

- the price;

- the promotional and selling activities;

- availability;

- service.

2.2 Maintaining customer satisfaction

All of the examples of elements in the marketing mix that we have looked at so far are to do with the initial 'offer' – they are things that count when the customer is making the decision to buy. However, there are other elements in the mix which affect the *long-term* loyalty of the customer, and these are extremely important for survival in the market, even if they do not influence a new customer's *initial* decision.

These elements are those which ensure continuing customer satisfaction.

Activity 13

■ Time guide 3 minutes

In the case of both the building society and the electronics firm, long-term customer loyalty may be vital for their survival. List *three* factors which could influence customers to stay with, or to desert their supplier:

_____

_____

_____

I think the first is the performance of the product.

If the analyser continually breaks down or under-performs, the customer is likely to become very disillusioned with the supplier.

If the deposit account turns out to offer lower interest and less flexible terms than other products, including new ones entering the market, the building society customer may close his or her account and switch to a competitor.

'Behind-the-scenes' factors also affect customer satisfaction, for example:

■ the speed at which the supplier's staff tackle problems and queries;

■ their attitude when doing so (which can vary from being eager to help to being downright hostile);

■ the general efficiency of the organization (including details like spelling the customer's name right; sending post or deliveries to the right address; getting financial details correct first time; keeping a record of conversations, messages and appointments).

2.3 Dealing with dissatisfaction

Problems and complaints are crucial in building the long-term marketing position of any organization. Naturally, it is a good idea to produce a quality product with a minimum of faults and errors, but no-one is perfect, and problems will occur in the most excellent of products. It is what happens after the customer has reported the problem that counts.

Here is an example.

Case Study

Tom rented a TV and video from Rapid Rentals Ltd. As part of the deal, they offered a refund if a repair took longer than 48 hours.

One day, the TV broke down, and Tom reported it. The following day, an engineer arrived and fixed it.

Three days later, it broke down again. The engineer came after two days and fixed it.

A week later, it broke down again. This time, the engineer did not come. After ten days, Tom complained in writing to the Managing Director of Rapid Rentals, and asked for the equipment to be removed and a refund given for the time it hadn't been working.

Tom received a very polite and apologetic letter from the MD, and the firm were prompt to remove the equipment and issue the refund. A few days later, however, a Tom received a letter from Rapid Rentals' accounts department, demanding a rental payment for equipment he no longer had. He returned this with a further letter to the MD. This time, the Customer Services Manager wrote back apologizing for the mix-up.

And that was the end of the matter – except that within days Tom received from the accounts department a new paying-in book for the following year!

Activity 14

■ Time guide 3 minutes

What would you say went wrong in the case of Tom and the rental firm?

_____

_____

_____

Clearly, the firm was badly organized: the left hand didn't know what the right hand was doing, and this always leads to problems. But organizational problems are the responsibility of the people in the organization:

■ someone should have noticed that this TV had broken down three times in rapid succession, and done something about it;

■ someone should have made sure that when the rental contract was cancelled, the accounts department were informed.

It always pays to keep an eye open for possible problems.

Activity 15

■ Time guide 2 minutes

No organization likes receiving complaints, but a number of leading companies now take the view that complaints can be positively beneficial in increasing customer loyalty. Try to suggest why this might be.

_____

_____

_____

_____

The logic goes like this:

■ some customers do not complain, they simply 'vote with their feet', i.e. they stop using us and go to a competitor next time;

■ the long-term attitude of those who do complain depends on how well we deal with the complaint; customers whose problem is promptly, efficiently and pleasantly solved, are likely to have *a higher opinion of us* than they did before the problem arose; they become more loyal, not less;

■ complaints are an important source of feedback about how well our product is performing; if we listen carefully and take the necessary measures, we can improve our product in the future.

Every single aspect of an organization that a customer encounters will have some impact on that customer's attitude, and therefore on his or her purchasing decisions.

It will either strengthen or weaken the organization's ability to succeed in the market place. The effect of any one element in the marketing mix may be quite small, but even a very small 'minus point' may be enough to let in a competitor whose 'package' is marginally more attractive.

In this 'total' approach, it is obvious that people and the way they deal with customers will be particularly important. Every employee whose activities have an effect on the product or the customer contributes to market success or failure. In fact, the most successful organizations believe that *everyone on their payroll* is part of the marketing mix.

Activity 16

■ Time guide 12 minutes

Here are four short descriptions of people working in quite different kinds of jobs. Think about each situation carefully, and then write down what you think about their impact on their organization's marketing mix.

Sarah was credit control supervisor with a large firm of builders' merchants. She and her team spent at least three days every month chasing customers for payment of overdue accounts. 'Be hard as nails with them,' she told the others. 'Be as nasty as you like. Just get the money. Every £1 overdue is making us less competitive.'

What sort of effect is this likely to have on this firm's position in the market?

_____

_____

_____

_____

Trevor and Marion were shelf-fillers in a supermarket. All they had to do was to re-stock shelves following detailed plans sent from Head Office. One day, a customer stopped and asked 'Can you tell me whereabouts the sponge fingers are, please?' The two looked at each other. Marion just shrugged and went on shelf-filling. Trevor said 'Sorry, dunno. You'll have to ask someone else.'

What do you think they should have done, and why?

_____

_____

_____

_____

continued overleaf

Peter, a section manager in a factory producing packaging materials, received a phone call from Sally, one of the sales representatives. 'Peter, sorry to trouble you, but I'm with a customer and we need some information. Can you confirm a list of tensile strengths in various gauges for us?' Peter was not pleased: 'Look, young lady, I haven't got time for that sort of thing. I've got production targets to meet here. If you wanted that sort of information you should have thought about it beforehand. Goodbye.' Sally apologized to her customer as best she could: 'Sorry, we've got one or two awkward types back at the factory.'

What does this episode tell you about this company, and what effect will the incident have on its attempts to sell its products?

_____

_____

_____

_____

Danny was a service engineer for the electricity company, and was allowed to take his van home at night. Almost every night he parked it in a spot which was very handy for him, but very inconvenient for some of his neighbours. There were numerous complaints.

Why should the electricity company be concerned about such a minor matter?

_____

_____

_____

_____

See whether you agree with my views.

■ Certainly, as Sarah says, poor credit control affects profitability, and hence competitiveness, but a firm's credit terms are also part of its marketing mix. Customers expect credit, and many firms expect to give it. At issue here is the manner in which Sarah approaches it. The right way is to be firm but reasonable: being 'nasty' to customers is neither necessary nor helpful. It almost certainly means that some customers will go elsewhere as soon as the opportunity arises. So Sarah may be doing more harm than good to the business.

■ Trevor and Marion think that they have nothing to do with 'the marketing approach' because their job is just to fill shelves. But they are visible to customers, and customers may well ask them questions: their appearance and behaviour are both part of the firm's marketing mix. This customer will not care what their particular job is: she only knows that they represent the supermarket, and that they are unhelpful, unfriendly and lacking in knowledge. Next time she shops, it may be elsewhere. Most retail firms now expect – and train – all their staff how to respond to customers' questions – and the minimum should be to say 'Sorry, I don't know, but I'll find out for you.'

■ Peter is a typical example of a production-oriented person. He needs to re-think his attitude, because if Sally can't sell Peter's output, all the production skills in the world will count for nothing. Furthermore, it is very bad practice to be unhelpful towards colleagues: the best organizations now insist not only that their customers should be treated with every consideration, *but that colleagues should be treated as customers!*

Sally makes things worse, by letting the customer see that she is irritated with Peter. The customer will not be impressed with the organization, and will have a lingering suspicion about its flexibility and willingness to help.

■ Danny works for a company which has a local monopoly. No matter how much he annoys the neighbours, they cannot get their electricity from someone else. But incidents like these damage a business's reputation. They may make customers more inclined to be difficult over all sorts of issues. And although they will continue to use electricity, when it comes to fitting a new cooker, they may choose gas; and if it is central heating, perhaps they will choose oil.

Sarah, Trevor, Marion, Peter and Danny were not in the front line of the marketing effort. But what they did and said, and how they did and said it, had an effect on their organization's marketing mix. It is important for everyone to recognize the following.

Everyone on the payroll affects the organization's competitiveness.

The way we approach our job, our colleagues and
our customers can either help or hinder the
marketing effort.

Self check 2

■ Time guide 6 minutes

1. Define what is meant by 'the marketing mix'.

_____

_____

_____

2. List *five* factors which usually form an important part of the marketing mix.

_____

_____

_____

_____

_____

continued overleaf

3. List *three* 'behind the scenes' factors that can affect long-term customer loyalty.

_____

_____

_____

Response check 2

1. The marketing mix is the sum total of all the elements that go to make up the 'offer' that an organization makes to its market.

2. The most important factors are usually:

   (a) the product itself;

   (b) the price;

   (c) the promotion and selling;

   (c) the availability;

   (d) the service.

   However, there are many other factors, any of which may play an important part in a particular case.

3. The three 'behind-the-scenes factors' that most affect long-term customer loyalty are:

   (a) the speed with which problems and complaints are tackled;

   (b) the attitude of the staff;

   (c) the general efficiency of the organization.

4	Summary

- The marketing mix is the sum total of all the factors that form part of the 'offer' that an organization makes to its market.

- Every organization has a slightly different marketing mix; otherwise it is difficult to find a competitive edge.

- There are many elements in the marketing mix, but the most important ones are usually:
  - the product itself;
  - the price;
  - the promotional and selling activities;
  - availability;
  - service.

- The marketing mix affects both the customer's initial buying decision and longer-term customer satisfaction, and hence loyalty. This depends largely upon:
  - the performance of the product;
  - behind the scenes factors, such as efficiency, service, and the attitude of the people involved.

- Customers who complain can become more loyal than before, provided their complaint is dealt with promptly and efficiently.

● The most successful market-led organizations believe that:

– everyone on the payroll is part of the marketing mix;

– colleagues should be treated with the same consideration as customers;

– the way we approach our job, our colleagues and our customers can either help or hinder our organization's marketing effort.

THE RIGHT PRODUCT AT THE RIGHT PRICE

1   Introduction

We have already seen that what counts is what the market wants, not what the supplier thinks it ought to want. Any organization that develops a product first, and then seeks a market for it second, is courting disaster.

There are many elements in the marketing mix, and among them the product itself is central. But there are also many different aspects to the product: quality, suitability, design, range and price. Failure to get any one of these right will also threaten the ability to compete.

Above all, the product has to be right for the particular part of the market at which it is aimed.

2   The product

Activity 17

■ Time guide 3 minutes

How does an organization know whether its product is meeting the needs of the market? Suggest *three* different ways of finding out:

_____

_____

_____

As we saw in Part A, there are three main ways of knowing whether a product (whether it is goods or services) is meeting the needs of its market. The first is simply to look at sales (or take-up, in the case of non-commercial organizations). If demand for the product is falling, it is not meeting the needs of the market as well as it did before.

The second source of knowledge is market research, which can help to show why demand is falling, and whether it is likely to go on doing so.

The third main indicator of how well the product is meeting its customers' needs is the level of complaints, returns, cancellations, and similar signs of dissatisfaction.

Many hard-working people are deeply hurt and puzzled when their products go into a decline. Often, they are so proud of their product that they cannot understand why customers are not buying it any longer. There is even a tendency to blame the customers: perhaps they have become less interested in quality, less loyal, even less intelligent.

Of course, this is a fundamental mistake. Change is in the market's very nature:

● the needs of customers change;

● the other products available in the market change;

● all products have a limited life, even if it is a relatively long one.

The market inevitably condemns every product to death, but that doesn't mean that its life cannot be prolonged. Indeed, the first reaction on seeing a product slipping down the charts should be to ask:

● why is it happening?

● what can we do about it?

Activity 18

■ Time guide 5 minutes

Grindleford Toys found that sales of their high quality cast-metal miniature cars were falling at around one percent per month.

Try to list *four* possible explanations for this decline.

_____

_____

_____

_____

I think that we can divide the many possible reasons into two groups: **external factors** and **internal factors**.

External factors

■ *Changed economic conditions*: if the economy generally has been in recession, all kinds of consumer spending may be affected. Luxury items, and high-quality toys may be in this category, are often the worst affected.

■ *Changed market conditions*: the market doesn't know that its needs have changed until someone offers a new product that will meet them. But when the right new product comes along it can suddenly wipe the floor with old-established and highly respected market leaders. In the 1950s, a large majority of toy cars were made of metal; today almost all are plastic, because plastic is a cheaper and easier material to work with. The traditional 'quality' manufacturers who resisted this trend have mostly gone out of business or been taken over.

The most likely explanation for the decline in Grindlefords' market is the arrival of new and highly competitive products.

Internal factors

It is always possible that internal factors such as the following are responsible for Grindlefords becoming less competitive in the market place.

Part
C

■ *Marketing factors*:
  – a failure to market and sell the products efficiently;
  – a failure to introduce enough new products to replace ageing ones.

■ *Management factors*:
  – financial mismanagement;
  – a failure to invest in more efficient machinery;
  – a failure to streamline working practices;
  – poor human relations resulting in interrupted production.

■ *Production factors*:
  – too many faults and errors in manufacture;
  – failure to operate at optimum capacity.

All these internal factors will make Grindlefords' product more costly to produce and therefore less competitive in the market place.

There is little we can do about external factors – we have to learn to live with them. But internal factors are a different matter.

An organization which wishes to keep up with the changing market must be constantly on its toes, and must be prepared to change its products and its methods of working too. The whole organization needs to be geared to the needs of the ever-changing market.

3   The product range

**3.1
Product range and
market segmentation**

In all consumer markets there are different segments. Often there are many, as with cars (most cars are aimed at particular market segments, such as retired people, managing directors, sales reps, women, boy racers, farmers, families etc.). In most markets, we can identify three broad segments, like this:

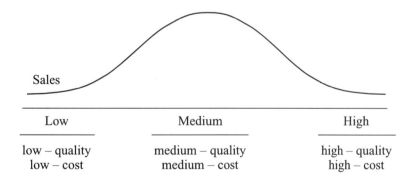

As you can see from the 'distribution curve', the biggest sales (for most consumer products at any rate) are in the middle ranges, and this is where competition is also highest, because the total sums of money involved here are much greater.

But there is a market at the top end too, producing fewer sales in total, but a relatively high cash income. Profits may also be relatively high.

We see the same sort of segmentation in many service industries, and restaurants are a good example.

Restaurant	Description	Market segment
'Le Chapeau Noir'	One of the top restaurants in the country, offering a wide range of individually prepared dishes cooked by internationally famous chefs. Situated in a pleasant rural location and with a very high standard of service.	*Top of the range:* • top quality; • maximum choice; • high prices; • small market.
'The Merry Chef Inn'	Part of a nationwide chain which offers a standardized menu at moderate prices and is organized for maximum cost-efficiency. Situated mainly in busy town centres, and providing a medium level of service.	*Middle of the range:* • middle quality; • limited choice; • competitive prices; • large market.
'Sid's Greasy Spoon Cafe'	A family run café/snack bar, offering tea, coffee and fried meals of the bacon, egg, sausage, chips and peas type. Situated on the edge of an industrial estate.	*Bottom of the range:* • low quality; • limited choice; • low prices; • limited market.

Activity 19

■ Time guide 5 minutes

The three different restaurants are clearly aimed at three different market segments, in that they aim to attract three entirely different types of customer. How would you describe the three different types of customer?

Le Chapeau Noir _____

_____

The Merry Chef _____

_____

Sid's Café _____

_____

One way of looking at the differences is by social class. Clearly, Sid's clientele are working class; the top of the range restaurant attracts the upper class; and the Merry Chef Inn is in between.

You may already know that the advertising and marketing industry often refers to these groups by a letter:

- A = professionals;
- B = managers and other senior grades;
- C1 = white collar workers.
- C2 = skilled manual workers;
- D = unskilled manual workers.

However, this is a very crude division, and it is becoming much more common to try to analyse consumers in a more sensitive way:

- by the area in which they live (for example through the Area Classification of Residential Neighbourhood or ACORN system);
- according to their tastes, interests and lifestyles (e.g. by finding out which newspapers they read, the type of holidays they take and the kind of cars they drive).

Either way, the two principal respects in which the segments differ are:

- the amount they have to spend;
- their needs in terms of quality.

Some restaurants are capable of competing in more than one segment of the market. Many Chinese restaurants, for example, have three different products aimed at three different segments of the Chinese food market:

- the cheap and basic 'business lunch' for office workers;
- the expensive sit-down meal (evenings only);
- the take-away service (a very varied range of customers).

So Chinese restaurants have a product range consisting of three products.

Activity 20

■ Time guide 2 minutes

Why is it to the advantage of a restaurant to compete in three separate market segments rather than just one? Note down **one** good reason.

_____

_____

It is a simple matter of economics. Restaurants have a particular set of resources – human skills, equipment etc. If they can utilize these resources in three market segments instead of one, they are both increasing their revenue and reducing their unit costs. It is far more profitable than concentrating on just one part of the market.

Much of manufacturing and commerce has the same approach to product range and market segments:

● furniture makers may produce everything from cheap self-assembly kits to hand-finished luxury items;

● car makers like Ford offer a large range from cheap Fiestas to expensive Granadas (and there is also an extensive range *within* each model);

● banks offer a range of savings and deposit accounts tailored to the needs of different income groups;

● publishers issue books ranging from cheap paperbacks to expensive scientific works.

As a general rule, the middle segments of a market are much larger than the top or bottom segments; they are also where the competition is fiercest.

Activity 21

■ Time guide 2 minutes

Think about the range of products which your own organization offers, using the same basic skills and other resources. See if you can identify the range under these headings:

Low quality/cost _____

_____

Mid quality/cost _____

_____

High quality/cost _____

_____

**3.2
Product range
and customer choice**

Simple economics is not the only reason for offering a range of products; it is also important to be able to offer the customer a choice.

Take a confectionery wholesaler which distributes its output to High Street retail shops.

To persuade the retailers to accept their product for sale, the wholesaler must be able to offer what the market wants. And what the market wants in this case is variety – a range of different types, flavours, colours and sizes from which to choose.

Any retailer with any sense will insist on the wholesaler supplying the full range of products, and maintaining their availability at all times. This will have a big impact on the way the wholesaler approaches its business, and in turn on the manufacturers from which it acquires its supplies.

Activity 22

■ Time guide 5 minutes

Suppose you want to buy someone a waterproof outdoor coat as a birthday present. Near where you live, but five miles apart, are two factory shops where you can buy the kind of coat you are looking for.

■ Factory A makes only one kind of outdoor coat. It is good value at £39.95, but is only available in green.

■ Factory B offers a range of coats, in a variety of styles and qualities, with prices ranging from £29.95 to £85.95.

If you had time to visit only one of the shops, which would you choose, and why?

_____

_____

_____

You may have had a particular reason for choosing Factory A, but I think most people would have plumped for Factory B. The reason must be obvious: choice. In this case:

■ a choice of prices;

■ a choice of qualities;

■ a choice of colours and styles.

Choice is a key concept in consumer marketing. Even when we buy something as ordinary as a dustbin we like to have a choice of colours, sizes, shapes and materials. The shop which can offer us the biggest range is more likely to see the colour of our money.

The same goes for cars: we want a choice of colours, finish, engine size and accessories. And even in business markets, such as for office furniture, computers, catering services and packaging materials, the customer appreciates being offered a choice, and is unlikely to be impressed by suppliers who do not offer it.

But giving the customers the choice they demand can be hard work for people throughout the supplying company. It usually means:

● manufacturing a range of lines – and thus more time and money spent on development, design, scheduling, setting up machines and so on;

● holding a range of stock – and thus more time and money spent on warehousing, keeping inventory records, recording stock movements and so on.

Activity 23

■ Time guide 4 minutes

Kirkwade's make a range of 50 different items of menswear. One item is an outdoor coat, style number C42. Last year's sales of C42 were 500. Of these, 200 were sold in October, and the remainder in small repeat orders over the following six months. This year, total sales are expected to be 550.

It is August, and three schedules for producing the coats are being considered:

1. Produce 225 immediately, and the remainder in monthly runs as orders come in.

2. Produce 275 immediately and a further 275 in November.

3. Produce 550 immediately.

If you were in charge of production, which schedule would you choose, and why?

_____

_____

A case could be made for each of the three schedules.

■ Option 1 looks attractive because it is 'safe' – producing what you know you can sell and then waiting for repeat orders to come in. However, it would be the most expensive option, because of the cost of starting and stopping small production runs. There would also be a continuing risk of running short of stock owing to a sudden demand, or production problems.

■ Option 2 would avoid some of the problems associated with Option 1, and is a good compromise between the cautious approach of Option 1 and the lower cost of Option 3.

■ Option 3 would be the cheapest in unit cost terms, but it leaves us with the problem of holding considerable stocks right through the winter. This will tie up both money (the value of the coats remaining unsold), space, and the time of stockroom staff.

It looks like either Option 2 or Option 3. The firm simply has to decide whether the extra production costs of Option 2 outweigh the extra storage and handling costs of Option 3.

Either way, the market is exerting its pressure:

● the coats must be produced at an ***economical price***;

● they must be available ***when the market wants them***.

We can sum up this section by saying that:

● it is vital to offer the market the right product;

● often this means providing a range of products so that the customer has choice;

● the stocks must be available when the customer wants them.

<table>
<tr><td>4</td><td>The right price</td></tr>
</table>

Of all the factors which make up the marketing mix, the price is usually the most important. At the time when I wrote this unit, the airline industry was in a very deep recession, and this was made worse by fear of terrorist attacks; as a result, the demand for trans-Atlantic flights was reduced by more than 60 per cent.

In order to stimulate demand, several airlines slashed fares to and from the USA by half. A spokesman explained that although people were not flying because they feared being blown up, there was a point when the price would fall so low that many would overcome their fear and grab a real bargain. Money talks: there would seem to be large numbers of passengers who would risk being blown up on a flight costing £150, but not on one costing £300!

In principle, anything will sell (i.e. there will be demand for anything) if the price falls low enough. Scrap metal is a case in point. Even a rusty and broken-down washing machine, which will never work again, can be sold for scrap for a small sum.

The problem with most goods and services is that the price has to be low enough to create a demand, but high enough to produce a profit, and it is difficult to get this right.

**4.1
Costing a product**

Activity 24

◼ Time guide 3 minutes

To produce a profit, the price of a product must be greater than the total costs involved in getting it to the customer. List *six* main types of cost which go into a product like Grindlefords' metal toys.

_____

_____

_____

_____

_____

_____

The main costs associated with a manufactured product are as follows.

◼ *Development costs*, including:

  – market research;

  – design and pre-production;

  – making dies and jigs;

  – test-runs.

◼ *Production costs*, including:

  – set-up costs;

  – materials (metal, paint, rubber);

  – components bought in;

  – packaging;

  – repairs and maintenance;

  – wages and salaries of production staff;

  – power.

■ *Overhead costs*, including:

- management costs;

- administrative costs (including wages and salaries of office staff);

- rent, rates etc.;

- lighting, heating etc.;

- telephone, post, fax etc.;

- insurance, legal fees etc.;

- training.

■ *Distribution and selling costs*, including:

- storage and transport costs;

- advertising and costs of promotional events;

- promotional literature;

- salaries of selling staff;

- travel and other expenses.

There may be many more incidental costs than I have listed, and there also has to be a margin for profit; and probably something for tax.

The simplest way to work out the price of a product is to add up all the anticipated costs and then add a percentage for profit. (The costing of service products is broadly similar, except that materials and 'production' costs are usually insignificant, while labour costs are considerably higher.)

This is the so-called 'cost plus' method. However, this method is based entirely on internal considerations, especially production; it takes no account whatsoever of the market.

**4.2
Pricing for the market**

Grindlefords worked out that a new model would cost £3.41 to make, on a production run of 10,000. Fifteen per cent would be added as a profit margin, bringing the price at which it could be supplied to retailers to £3.92. Retailers would then add their own margin, and the model would probably appear in the shops at £4.99.

Activity 25

■ Time guide 3 minutes

Perhaps this is not the right price for the product. What other considerations would Grindlefords have to bear in mind when setting a price? Try to think of *two*.

_____

_____

The price may be right from Grindlefords' point of view, but is it right for the market? They need to consider how it compares with the prices of competing products. If the competition sells at £3.99, how can this product sell at £4.99?

A market-led firm would have approached this from a different angle: 'At what price can we sell this product? OK, now how can we produce the product at that price?'

If the answer is 'We can't', then it is a waste of time and money even trying.

On the other hand, perhaps the product is considerably cheaper than the competition, in which case limiting the mark-up for gross profit to 15 per cent seems unduly modest. If it is capable of earning 25 per cent, why shouldn't it do so?

Activity 26

■ Time guide 3 minutes

There is no reason in principle why Grindlefords' products should not sell, at a higher price, in the top segment of the market, provided they are right for that segment. What would 'right' be in this context?

_____

_____

_____

_____

Products that survive in the upper end of the market have to have something about them which justifies the higher price, for example:

■ superior quality and durability;

■ a high reputation and a quality brand name;

■ superior style and fashion.

In other words, it has to be a 'premium product'.

But what if our toy makers can't claim premium product status? Clearly they have two options:

● either give up and try something else;

● or cut costs.

Activity 27

■ Time guide 6 minutes

Grindlefords' Managing Director decided that costs would have to be cut in order for the firm to compete, but that they couldn't afford to reduce the costs associated with selling and marketing.

Look at the list of costs below, and try to suggest *two* ways of reducing costs in (a) production and (b) overheads:

■ market research;

■ design and pre-production;

■ making dies and jigs;

■ test-runs;

■ set-up costs;

■ materials (metal, paint, rubber);

■ components bought in;

■ packaging;

■ repairs and maintenance;

■ wages and salaries of production staff;

■ power;

■ management costs;

■ administrative costs (including wages and salaries of office staff);

■ rent, rates etc.;

■ lighting, heating etc.;

■ telephone, post, fax etc.;

■ insurance, legal fees etc.;

■ training;

■ storage and transport costs;

■ advertising and costs of promotional events;

■ promotional literature;

■ salaries of selling staff;

■ travel and other expenses.

Production cost reductions

_____

_____

Overheads

_____

_____

On the production side, there are some things that could be done immediately, such as reducing wastage. This might involve:

- monitoring current levels of wastage and identifying the reasons for it (wastage means wasted time and labour as well as wasted materials);

- spending more time setting up machines properly before starting a production run;

- spending more time on training operatives (it is a strange fact that training is often one of the first things to be cut when an organization starts to reduce its costs – and this is very counter-productive in the long run);

- ensuring greater care is taken when handling materials and equipment of all kinds;

- being more careful with paperwork, so that there are fewer misunderstandings and errors;

- being more careful about stocks and inventory, avoiding over-ordering and making more frequent checks.

On the overheads side, all sorts of reductions must be possible. Perhaps the MD could spend a little less on business lunches! Telephone and fax costs can be reduced by better organization and by making calls at cheaper rates. Savings can also usually be made on lighting and heating, without making working conditions more difficult or uncomfortable.

However, although economy measures of this kind are useful in improving an organization's financial performance, there is seldom enough scope to make a real difference to prices in the market by these means.

To make a product more competitive, major changes in the efficiency of the business are needed.

Activity 28

- Time guide 5 minutes

Suggest *two* ways in which a firm like Grindlefords' could reduce the production costs of its products by a very large amount – say 40 per cent.

_____

_____

_____

_____

The answer that usually springs to mind is 'getting the workforce to work harder', or 'cutting wages all round', but this is the wrong approach. Cutting wages, in particular, seldom produces the desired results – though it can cause an awful lot of problems.

Certainly, it will be useful if staff could work a bit harder. But this again is not the real answer: most people work reasonably hard, and it is not realistic to expect someone to, say, make 40 per cent more physical movements than they currently do.

A more effective approach is to look at the way work is organized. For example, flexibility between people doing different jobs is important. If there are only two people in the firm who understand the computer, and one falls ill while the other is away on holiday, that is a problem. Similarly on the factory floor: if only one person can set up precision machinery properly, that is bound to hold up production at some point.

Major innovations in working practices may have to be considered too:

- double shift working;

- introducing quality circles;

- changing methods of paying staff;

- incentives for acquiring additional skills;

- flexible working hours.

All of these can have important effects on productivity, and thus reduce costs, but the biggest gains can only be made by investing in new and more efficient machinery.

When an organization invests in new equipment, the cost is often enormous, but there should be two important benefits:

- considerably increased output at lower staffing levels;

- reduced unit production costs.

Activity 29

■ Time guide 4 minutes

There are benefits for the organization and its shareholders, but what impact is a major investment programme and increased productivity likely to have on the workforce?

_____

_____

_____

This pattern of investment, new product development and changing working practices is forced on organizations by the market. It has enormous implications for supervisors at all levels because it means change, and change can create resentment and insecurity among the workforce.

This applies in the office as much as on the factory floor: a secretary with a computer can produce as much as two secretaries with electric typewriters, or four with manual machines. An organization which is prepared to equip all its managers, administrators and specialists with networked computer terminals can do without secretaries altogether.

The market talks loud and clear to organizations about how they need to conduct themselves. Supervisors in particular need to understand these issues so that they can lead their teams through the constant changes that the market demands.

As we have seen, the quality of a product:

● is clearly part of the marketing mix;

● is closely related to the price which can be charged.

However, this does not mean that every product has to be of the highest possible quality. If that was true, all cars would have to be Rolls Royces.

What it does mean is that the quality has to be right for the price charged. This explains why in most markets we find a range of goods which do the same job but at different levels of price and sophistication. It also accounts for the fact that customers do not expect Rolls Royce standards from a Skoda, but can still be perfectly happy with the Skoda.

Problems arise when the quality falls below **what the customer expects for the price** paid, and when the back-up services do not meet the customer's expectations.

**5.1
Maintaining standards
of quality**

Case
Study

Lee & Sherrins, a leading food manufacturer, were able to buy ground almonds from a number of countries and via various different suppliers, with very little variation in price. As it happened, they normally bought them from Turkey, through a supplier with whom they had a good relationship. Then problems began to arise. One consignment had to be rejected because it was contaminated with chlorine. Next the colour of the product changed from white to a pale beige. Finally, there were hold-ups when the supplier was unable to deliver on time.

L&S were reluctant to abandon their old-established supplier, and pressed them for guarantees of quality and supply for the future, but these did not halt the problems. So they simply switched to another source, and the original supplier lost the account, even though they offered to drop the price.

Activity 30

■ Time guide 2 minutes

Contracts can easily be lost owing to production problems. What would you say were the supplier's *two* major shortcomings?

_____

_____

_____

_____

First, they did not monitor the production quality properly. Someone must have known that the quality was falling, but nothing was done about it. Secondly, they failed to meet the customer's delivery dates. It is easy for suppliers to become sloppy about this, but if the customer needs everything exactly at the right time in order to start a production run, then it is a major problem.

There was also a third problem: the supplier did not put things right when the customer complained.

Quality usually means reliability too. Lee & Sherrins' original supplier lost their contract because their reliability broke down. To understand how important this is, we need to think about what the customer needs.

Activity 31

■ Time guide 2 minutes

Put yourself in the position of the customer. Which of these would you think is the more reliable product? (You can assume that price, delivery and so on are similar for both.)

■ Product A has been the same for many years, and you've never had any serious complaints, so you haven't had anything to do with the manufacturer and couldn't comment on how efficiently the factory is run.

■ Product B tends to vary and sometimes doesn't meet your specifications. On several occasions this has caused you serious problems, but the supplier is always very helpful and apologetic, and usually manages to put things right – in the end.

As far as reliability is concerned, most customers would prefer Product A. They may have their problems and their ups and downs, but they certainly don't show it. This suggests that they think ahead, and spot possible problems before they become serious.

One aspect of this is putting a great deal of effort into monitoring standards.

Activity 32

■ Time guide 2 minutes

Suppose that you were the supervisor responsible for quality control at Lee & Sherrins.

The buyers have found a new supplier for ground almonds. It may turn out to be a reliable source, it may not. Jot down *three* items of information that it would be worth recording, so as to keep a long-term check.

_____

_____

_____

You would want to record whether the product met the specifications in terms of colour, flavour, aroma, purity, etc.

You would also check that the quantities were right, and that the deliveries came at the right time, in the right packaging.

Most well-organized buyers keep records of this kind.

5.2
The quality of service products

The nature of the product offered by service-based organizations is also important. For example, British Rail has had many critics for many reasons, but one particular area of complaint used to be Passenger Enquiries. People phoning up to check train times often had to wait for long periods before getting an answer. Sometimes the phone seemed permanently engaged, sometimes it just rang and rang – in fact it was common for customers to give up in disgust. When the phone was answered, the people at the other end often seemed brusque and unhelpful.

I don't know the details, but I am sure that the enquiry staff themselves were pretty unhappy: feeling overworked, understaffed and generally misunderstood. They probably felt they were doing their best to provide a decent service, but that customers didn't appreciate the difficulties they faced.

Activity 33

■ Time guide 2 minutes

What do you think could be done to improve a service of that kind?

_____

_____

_____

If your answer was to increase staffing levels, install more lines and train the enquiry staff to be more friendly and helpful, then you are right, because that is what BR did. Now a service which was a constant irritant to customers has become a cause for much praise – a very positive element in BR's marketing mix.

And why was the improvement made? Simply because the people concerned started to look at it from the customer's point of view.

There is an important lesson here:

> customers are not interested in your problems – they simply want the right product at the right time.

Here is another example of how the quality of service affects the customer's attitude.

Case Study

Janet was office supervisor for a firm of accountants. One Monday morning in January she found that the word processor used for important correspondence would not work.

The senior partner wanted three important letters which he had dictated over the weekend to be done immediately. Janet thumbed through the Yellow Pages and came up with two local firms which repaired office machines.

She phoned Company A and tried to explain her problem. An uninterested voice interrupted her to say:

'Don't worry, it's the cold you know. It'll sort itself out. Give us a ring back at lunchtime if it doesn't and we'll see what we can do.'

Janet then phoned Company B. An interested voice assured her that they would be able to help, and then listened while she explained her problem.

'It's probably not a serious fault, just the cold weather. Some machines can be affected like that. Try and get some heat onto the machine – just gentle heat or you may do some damage. In the meantime I'll re-route one of our service engineers, so there should be someone there within the hour.

Activity 34

■ Time guide 3 minutes

Write down a few of the words that you might use to describe Company A, and a few of the words you might use to describe Company B.

Company A _____

_____

Company B _____

_____

My guess is that you would use words much like these.

■ For Company A: inefficient, couldn't-care-less, useless, disorganized, sloppy, on-the-way-out.

■ For Company B: efficient, helpful, concerned, organized, keen, on-the-way-up.

If you are involved in the production, delivery, or quality control of any product of anykind, think carefully about this issue.

What can *you* do:

● to make sure your product meets the customer's needs in terms of quality?

● to make sure your product reaches the customer on time?

Self check 3

■ Time guide 8 minutes

1. List *two* external factors which can reduce an organization's competitiveness:

_____

_____

2. Complete this sentence in your own words:

The selling price of a product has to be low enough _____ but high enough _____.

3. Explain what is meant by 'a segment of the market'.

_____

_____

_____

4. Describe the cost-plus method of costing a product.

_____

_____

_____

continued overleaf

5. What is the main shortcoming of the cost-plus method?

_____

_____

_____

Response check 3

1. Among the external factors which can reduce competitiveness are:

(a) changed economic conditions (recession etc.);

(b) changed market conditions (new competitors, new competing products).

2. The selling price of a product has to be low enough TO SELL (MAKE IT COMPETITIVE etc.) but high enough TO MAKE A PROFIT.

3. A segment of the market is a particular part, defined by the quality and price of the products which sell there, and the needs and spending habits of the customers within it.

4. The cost-plus method consists of first estimating and then adding up all the costs involved in producing the product, then adding a percentage for profit.

5. The main shortcoming of the method is that it takes no account of what the market is prepared to pay.

6   Summary

- All products have a limited life-cycle, but their useful life can be prolonged.

- A product's decline may be due to:

  - external factors (changed economic or market conditions);

  - internal factors (such as inefficiency or lack of investment).

- Most organizations try to offer a range of products to the market. This brings in extra revenues by using the same basic skills and material resources.

- The range of products is designed to match different segments of the market, which are defined mainly by:

  - the amount they have to spend;

  - their needs in terms of quality.

- All things being equal, customers tend to prefer the supplier who offers them the widest choice. This is another reason for offering a range of products.

- Anything will sell if the price falls low enough. The art of pricing is to set a price which is:

  - high enough to make a profit;

  - low enough to create a demand.

- The simplest method of working out the price of a product is to add up all the costs involved and then add a margin for profit. This is the cost-plus method.

- The problem with this method is that it takes no account of what the market is prepared to pay.

- High-priced products can still sell, provided that they can justify being a premium product.

- In general, the need to compete in an ever-changing market means a constant search for ways of cutting unit costs.

- Economy measures are useful, and so is getting people to work harder; but large-scale cost reductions require:

  – investment;

  – changed working practices.

- These changes present supervisors with many challenges.

- Maintaining a consistent quality is vital for success in the market.

- Customers prefer a reliable product from a reliable supplier.

- Quality and consistency are just as important for organizations whose products are services.

THE RIGHT PLACE, THE RIGHT TIME AND THE RIGHT WAY

1   Introduction

Suppose we have the right product at the right price, but we offer it to the market a year late (or just as bad, a year early). Obviously, we will miss the boat.

On the other hand, suppose we have the right product, at the right price *and* at the right time, but we launch it in East Anglia only, when the real market is the whole of Northern Europe. Again, we will miss the boat.

These two suppositions may be extreme, but it is surprising how often organizations fail to hit the right time and place for their products. There may be all sorts of reasons for this, from failure to study the market accurately, to production problems, to sheer bad luck. But whatever the reason, the upshot is a disaster.

In this part of the unit, we are going to see why the right place and time are so crucial, and look at some of the things that organizations, and that means the people in them, can do to make sure things go right.

2   The right place

Some of us may have had cereal for breakfast, or perhaps a cup of coffee and a slice of toast. Whatever it was, we did not produce these things ourselves. The raw materials probably came from overseas, perhaps from the other side of the globe, and even the factory that processed them may have been hundreds of miles away. In order for us to buy them, they had to be brought to a place where we could conveniently do so.

The same applies to the customers who buy the products that we ourselves supply.

Making sure that goods and services are available when we want to buy them is part of marketing, and comes under the general heading of *distribution*.

We can think of distribution in two main ways:

- the chain of distribution;
- physical distribution.

These obviously refer to goods rather than services, but the distribution of service products is also an issue, as we shall see. So too is the storage and handling of the stocks prior to delivery.

The 'chain of production and distribution' looks like this:

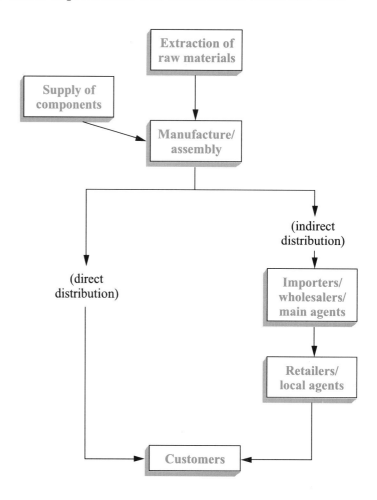

This chain may have few links or many, but if even one of them
fails, the customer's needs will not be met, and he or she will go
elsewhere.

2.2
**Stock handling
and storage**

Since warehousing plays an important part in the chain of
distribution, the efficiency of stock handling and storage obviously
affects the ability to supply the right product at the right time and
place.

Here is an example of what can go wrong.

*Mary, the supervisor in an office equipment company, received an order
for a white leather executive chair, reference number 2140. She checked
with the stock records, which showed one such chair in stock.*

*Mary passed the order down to the warehouse supervisor, who phoned
back to say that bin 2140 was empty. As the order was for urgent
delivery, the customer cancelled it.*

*Later that day, Mary was walking through the warehouse on her way
to the canteen, when she spotted what she thought was a white leather
chair type 2140 perched on top of a bin containing desks. She had a
word with one of the warehousemen, who explained that he'd put the
chair there three weeks previously because bin 2140 was full at the
time.*

Activity 35

■ Time guide 3 minutes

What was the problem in this case, and who was responsible?

_____

_____

_____

The problem was lack of communication – the warehouseman didn't communicate what he had done. But the responsibility was the supervisor's – for not ensuring that his staff realized they **needed** to communicate about such things, perhaps for not encouraging an atmosphere in which people were **willing** to communicate, and certainly for not carrying out spot checks on bin contents.

This incident illustrates just some of the problems of place and time which arise every day in the handling, storage and control of stock. The supervisor is often the person best able to solve these problems.

It's no good producing the right product at the right price, if we cannot get it to the customer at the right time.

**2.3
Physical distribution**

Then there is the transport side, physical distribution: the process of sending the products down the chain from one location to another, till they reach the customer.

Physical delivery of the product is an extremely important part of the marketing mix. Indeed, under contract law, the buyer has the right to make delivery terms a condition of the contract; and if the delivery is late, they can refuse payment and even sue for damages.

Of course, losing a valued customer is even more serious.

In recent years, customers' delivery needs have tightened up. Many manufacturers and retailers now operate a 'just-in-time' system for deliveries of goods. This means that the goods should be timed to arrive just before they are needed, no later, and never much earlier. Thus supermarkets expect that delivery vans will arrive at a particular time, so that their staff can be ready to check the goods, and move them straight onto the shelves on the shop floor.

Manufacturers expect parts and sub-assemblies to arrive precisely when they are needed on the assembly line.

Activity 36

■ Time guide 4 minutes

What do you think is the main advantage which retailers and manufacturers get from the just-in-time system? Write your ideas down here.

_____

_____

_____

The principal advantage for the customer is not having to hold more than a very small amount of stock. Stock costs money, and it needs space to house it and people to look after it. It also ties up money until the moment when the stock is actually sold.

Activity 37

■ Time guide 3 minutes

What disadvantages does a just-in-time delivery system have for the supplier? Write down *two* suggestions:

_____

_____

The kind of customers we have been talking about work long hours and have a high throughput, so one problem is that they may require deliveries to be made at any time of day or night. This means that the supplier's staff, and especially despatch staff and drivers, also have to match these hours, which may be inconvenient for them.

Also it means that in effect the supplier does the warehousing for the customer, and thus carries the cost of that operation.

Thirdly, the system means more frequent but often smaller deliveries, because the customer is no longer prepared to store more than a minimum of stock.

Suppliers often grumble about all this, but at the end of the day they have no choice. There is always competition, and if one supplier cannot, or will not, deliver the product at the right place and the right time, then someone else certainly will.

Meeting delivery needs within the narrow time-frame often demanded, calls for hard work and attention to detail.

Activity 38

■ Time guide 5 minutes

Samuelsons produce hot pre-packed meals, which they distribute to offices, shops and factories over a wide area, using a small fleet of vans. Orders are accepted up to 11am on the day they are required, and all orders are delivered by arrangement between 12 noon and 2pm.

Jot down *four* of the things that Samuelsons would have to do to make sure that their customers got what they wanted at the right time and place.

(Don't worry about the product itself – you can assume they have got the raw materials, equipment and so on.)

_____

_____

_____

_____

You may have included all sorts of things, because all sorts of things could go wrong with a time-sensitive operation like this. My suggestions are:

■ ensure that all orders have correct consignment notes so that they go to the right address;

■ double-check that each consignment is actually what the customer ordered;

■ make sure the orders are properly packed so that they don't get broken or damaged;

■ plan the most effective routes for the vehicles;

■ make sure the drivers understand what to do;

■ make sure the vehicles are regularly serviced and repaired so as to minimize the risk of breakdowns;

■ make sure the vehicles meet legal requirements so that they aren't kept off the road unnecessarily;

■ make sure there is a vehicle and driver on stand-by in case of emergencies.

Similar points will apply to almost any organization which operates a distribution service. The service has to be economical, but also reliable; customers soon get tired of receiving their orders late or not at all!

Although I asked you to ignore the production side in Activity 38, it is obviously an important issue. Many products are not available immediately, but have to be manufactured, imported, or 'customized' to order. This means that there has to be a 'lead time' between the customer placing the order and the product being delivered.

Some customers plan well ahead and allow plenty of lead time, but others are always in a hurry, and even in the best-planned organizations, emergencies can occur. So the supplier who can deliver the product soonest often has a distinct competitive edge.

**2.4
Distribution of
services**

Service-based organizations are not necessarily concerned with distributing goods; but they do have to make sure that the service they offer is distributed to the customer. A healthcare organization, for example, needs to ensure that its product is made available to everyone in its catchment area, and that they can gain access to it with the minimum of difficulty.

Activity 39

■ Time guide 4 minutes

Wetlands District Council's customers are the people who live and work in the district. It provides them with numerous services, such as refuse collection, street lighting, road maintenance, council housing, housing benefits and schools.

What would be involved in making a service like housing benefit advice available at the right place and time? Write down *two* or *three* suggestions.

_____

_____

_____

Assuming that the customers know that the service exists (a matter of promotion and advertising), the next step is to make it easy for them to gain access to it. In recent years, councils have tried to achieve this by such means as:

■ having free telephone 'advice-lines' for use by the public;

■ offering advice outside normal hours, for example in the evening and at weekends;

■ breaking up the housing department into smaller units, and siting these locally, near where the tenants actually live;

■ fitting out lorries or buses as mobile advice centres, and touring the localities on pre-advertised dates;

■ sending council officers to visit customers in their homes.

This is not yet universal, but it is a clear sign that local authorities are adopting a marketing approach towards the services they supply.

3 The right time

Time often gives one supplier the competitive edge. Recently, I bought a computer myself. This is how I decided among the 20 or so possible suppliers:

● I worked out the exact specifications that I wanted;

● I listed the suppliers who could provide exactly that;

● I checked their prices, and chose the three cheapest;

● I then checked how soon they could deliver, and chose the quickest.

All other things being equal, the time factor gave one supplier the competitive edge (and I'm pleased to say that the computer arrived exactly when they promised). Clearly, this firm was well-managed and well-organized, and everyone working there gave top priority to the customer's needs.

Activity 40

■ Time guide 5 minutes

Wetlands District Council was seeking tenders for the installation of a new computer system in its main offices. It shortlisted three different suppliers.

Supplier A was cheap, but would need 'about nine months' to complete the installation.

Supplier B was mid-priced, and would also need nine months to complete the installation; but gave a cast-iron guarantee that the work would be completed on time.

Supplier C was more expensive, but offered to complete the work in seven months.

Which one would you choose, all other things being equal? Give the reasons for your choice.

_____

_____

_____

A difficult choice, because we do not know how much weight this customer would place on time, as opposed to money. On the whole, I would plump for Supplier B, because I think it is better to be **sure** about completion within a given time than **unsure** about a somewhat earlier time.

Activity 41

■ Time guide 4 minutes

Joyce was quality control supervisor on a production line which made stereo loudspeakers. One day the sales manager came in and told her that batch number 9/93 (50 pairs of speakers for export) must be ready by 4pm the following day, as they had to be delivered to the airport six hours later. (This was three whole days ahead of the normal schedule.)

When the sales manager had gone, Joyce said to Harry, her line manager, 'Sales have gone and done it again, Harry. All they do is promise customers ridiculous deadlines, and to hell with everything else.'

We've all heard comments like that before. What points would you make to Joyce if you were Harry? Write your thoughts down in **one** or **two** sentences.

_____

_____

_____

_____

_____

An agreed delivery date is almost always a condition of an order, and sometimes it is the most important condition. Sometimes it is impossible to get the order without being prepared to offer an ultra-short lead time.

Of course, it is always possible for the sales team simply to tell their customer, 'Sorry – we can't do it in the time. It'll mean messing up our routine.'

But that is a very plain message to the customer that their order isn't important enough to bother with: next time that customer will go elsewhere.

The need to supply our products at the right time affects the way we organize our work, especially where demand fluctuates through the year.

Activity 42

■ Time guide 3 minutes

Imagine you have two friends, both of whom are sales people. John sells soap powder, and Mary sells children's toys. Write down what you think will be the biggest difference between their working lives.

_____

_____

There are several differences you might have written down – for example, toys are a varied product, while soap powder stays much the same year in year out.

The biggest difference, though, is 'seasonality'. Soap powder sells steadily all year round, so John will have a steady routine that will not vary much from month to month. Children's toys, on the other hand, are highly seasonal: almost 60 per cent of all toys are sold in the pre-Christmas period; sales in the rest of the year are rather low.

This means that Mary's activities will be quite different at different times of year; in particular, she will be extremely busy in the middle of the year, when retailers are placing their Christmas orders.

Seasonal demand will also influence the way that the manufacturers organize their work, as we saw earlier in the case of the outdoor coats. Anyone who makes seasonal products is likely to find themselves under a great deal of pressure at certain peak times. But it's essential to meet the challenge: otherwise, yet again, a competitor will do so.

Activity 43

■ Time guide 6 minutes

Write down a list of *ten* products for which demand is highly seasonal.

_____

_____

_____

_____

_____

_____

_____

_____

_____

_____

_____

You no doubt thought of all sorts of things which relate to Christmas, from puddings to wrapping paper. Easter eggs and fireworks are examples of the same kind of thing. But jewellery is also very seasonal, for the same reasons as toys. And there are also definite seasonal peaks in demand for:

- patio sets;
- lawnmowers;
- seeds and fertilizer;
- caravans;
- camping equipment;
- sunglasses;
- suntan lotion;
- swimwear;
- outdoor coats;
- gloves;
- bicycles;
- antifreeze;
- coal.

Actually, the list is endless, and market research plus experience will tell those concerned quite clearly when the peaks are to be expected.

However, there can still be unpredictable surges (or slumps) in demand, plus special priority orders of the type we described in Activity 41.

It may be annoying when it happens, but everyone needs to understand that in the furiously competitive world in which we work, our jobs depend on getting the product there on time – and the person who decides what is meant by 'on time' is the customer!

The production side must meet the needs of the customer, not the other way round. That is the essence of the marketing approach. If any organization finds that too inconvenient, a competitor will step in.

4   The right way: promotion and selling

Promotion and selling are the 'sharp end' of the marketing process. In fact, these are the activities that most people think of first when they hear the word marketing. Of course, we have seen in this Unit that marketing is a much wider concept, but that does not diminish the importance of 'the right way'.

We may well deliver the right product at the right price to the right place at the right time, but it will not be alone in that market place. Skilful competitors will have their own products there, and their marketing mix, though no doubt different from ours, may also have its attractions to the customer.

At this stage, the last competitive edge that we have is the skill and initiative of our promotional and selling people.

**4.1
Promotion**

In broad terms, both promotion and selling follow the AIDA strategy. This stands for the processes involved in persuading the customer to buy our product rather than another:

- getting their   **A**ttention;

- arousing their   **I**nterest in the product;

- stimulating a   **D**esire to acquire it;

- turning desire into   **A**ction, i.e. a sale.

What I mean by promotion is:

publicizing the organization's goods and services
so as to create an interest.

The techniques used include:

- advertising;

- preparing promotional literature;

- organizing promotional activities;

- public relations, and so on.

All these are methods of communication, and their purpose is to inform the customers about these goods and services, and to attract their interest.

Extension 3 Promotion is a specialized subject demanding specialized skills, and it is outside the scope of this unit. If you would like to find out more about the subject, I suggest that you consider taking up this extension.

What I mean by selling is:

using personal skills to turn interest into action (a sale).

**4.2
Selling – the retail
sector**

Many of us may think of selling as a specialist role, about which those of us not directly involved don't have to worry too much.

Perhaps this is true in some organizations, but there are many cases where it isn't.

Take retailing. Nearly one person in eight works in retailing, and many of them are directly responsible for selling. Of course this takes different forms:

- the way the goods are displayed is part of selling (it is called merchandizing, or sometimes 'silent selling');

- some retail sales staff are expected to sell actively, by going up to every customer who enters and working through a sales routine;

- others are expected to wait until a customer approaches them for help, and then to encourage them (a) to buy, (b) if possible to buy more, or something more expensive;

- the majority do not sell actively, but are expected to help the customer to buy, by being helpful, giving correct information, and so on.

Activity 44

■ Time guide 3 minutes

If you have never worked in retailing you may not have realized that these different selling strategies existed, but if you think about your own experiences as a shopper, you will soon recognize them. Try to give *one* example of each of the following types of retail firm.

■ In Type 1, staff sell actively by approaching customers.

_____

■ In Type 2, staff sell, but only after customers approach them.

_____

■ In Type 3, staff only have to help customers buy.

_____

■ Examples of Type 1 include many furniture stores, some shoe shops, and many hi-fi specialists.

■ Examples of Type 2 include department stores and firms like Woolworths.

■ Examples of Type 3 include self-service stores, especially supermarkets.

Obviously, supervisors have a key role to play in all three situations, because they are responsible for giving a good example and making sure that the sales staff perform their selling tasks effectively.

**4.3
Selling – the
salesforce method**

But what about all those organizations where the selling is done by 'sales reps' who go 'out on the road'? These are the industrial, commercial and service firms which mainly sell direct to other organizations, usually via a mobile salesforce.

Activity 45

■ Time guide 3 minutes

What can a team supervisor in an office cleaning firm do to back up the efforts of the sales reps as they visit potential clients?

_____

_____

_____

_____

Back-up might take many forms:

■ the reps may need information, as in the example in Activity 16;

■ they may need schedules or price lists posted out;

■ they may want a supervisor to talk directly to the customer about some technical or procedural point.

At some stage, the customer will often want to talk directly to the workteam, to try and judge how skilled and reliable they are. And the supervisor is highly likely to be involved in this.

But there is also a general point to make here: whenever you are in contact with people outside your organization, whether these are customers or not, you should always try to give the best possible impression.

Extension 4 This extension will tell you much more about many aspects of selling, including ways of using routine customer contacts so as to turn them into sales.

**4.4
Selling in the
broadest sense**

This returns us to the central issue of this unit – the idea that in a modern, market-led organization, everyone on the payroll is part of the marketing mix, and that everyone can either help or hinder the marketing effort.

What do you do to 'sell' your organization? In the broadest possible sense we are all responsible for selling our organization, by:

● helping to give it a good public image by our own behaviour;

● taking every opportunity to help the marketing effort;

● being positive about the product;

● being supportive of the efforts of colleagues to develop the business.

In the world of the competitive market, it's the only way to survive.

■ Time guide 6 minutes

Indicate whether the following statements are TRUE or FALSE:

1. Distribution is a technical matter and has nothing to do with the marketing approach. TRUE/FALSE.

2. The chain of distribution can have many links or few. TRUE/FALSE

3. Just-in-time delivery systems are highly inconvenient for the supplier, and should be avoided. TRUE/FALSE

4. Time is seldom a crucial part of the marketing mix because most customers allow plenty of lead time. TRUE/FALSE

5. The old saying 'time is money' has little meaning today. TRUE/FALSE

6. Distribution is not really an issue for service-type products such as security, office cleaning and insurance. TRUE/FALSE

7. The right place is always more important than the right time, in terms of the marketing mix. TRUE/FALSE

8. Customers should be realistic about delivery lead times, and accept that producers can't keep disrupting production plans for their benefit. TRUE/FALSE

9. Promotion is a specialized activity which is best left to the specialists. TRUE/FALSE

10. Everyone in an organization can help its sales effort. TRUE/FALSE

Response check 4

1. FALSE: the ability to provide the product at the right place and time is a crucial part of the marketing mix.

2. TRUE: in its simplest form, the chain might consist of a producer selling direct to the customer – for example a farm shop, or a craft workshop selling by mail order. Major multinational manufacturers, on the other hand, may have an immensely complex chain of distribution.

3. Inconvenient they may be, but it is FALSE to say they should be avoided. If this is what the market wants, suppliers must be prepared to provide it – or their competitors will.

4. FALSE: time is often crucially important; first, suppliers must be able to supply at the agreed dates and times; second, when all other things are equal, the supplier which can provide the product soonest often wins the order.

5. FALSE: time is money. Wasted time costs money, just as wasted materials do; and time is often the key factor in whether an order is won or lost.

6. FALSE: service organizations also have to ensure that their product is distributed to where the customer can most conveniently obtain it.

7. FALSE: whether place or time is more important depends entirely on the circumstances.

8. While regular customer would usually come to terms with their suppliers' operational needs, in a competitive situation, the customer's needs must always over-ride those of the supplier. Thus this statement is FALSE.

9. TRUE: though that does not mean that supervisors elsewhere in the organization can afford to ignore it.

10. TRUE – and this has been the theme of this entire unit.

- It is no good having the right product at the right price if it isn't made available at the right place and the right time.

- The mechanism for getting manufactured products to the customer at the right place and time is the chain of production and distribution, which includes:

  – stock handling and storage;

  – physical distribution.

- Customers are becoming more demanding in terms of distribution and delivery.

- Service products also have to be distributed to the customer, though the means of doing so are different.

- Time is often a decisive element in the marketing mix.

- Responsibility for ensuring that the product reaches the customer at the right place and time is shared by everybody working in:

  – sales;

  – administration;

  – production;

  – distribution.

- Supervisors have a particular responsibility to ensure that all their staff work towards this goal.

- Promotion and selling are the final important elements in the marketing mix. They provide the competitive edge when a number of equally good products confront each other in the market place.

- Promotion is about using techniques of advertising etc. to attract the customers' attention and arouse their interest.

- Selling is about personal skills to turn the customers' interest into action (i.e. a sale).

- Large numbers of people work directly in selling – especially in retailing.

- In organizations where the selling is carried out by a specialized salesforce, other staff can still assist and provide backup.

- In the last analysis, in an organization that adopts the marketing approach, everyone has a role to play in helping the product to succeed.

1   Quick quiz

Well done – you have completed the unit. Now listen to the questions on Side one of the audio cassette. If you are not sure about some of the answers, check back in the workbook before making up your mind.

Write down your answers in the space below.

1 _____

  _____

2 _____

  _____

3 _____

  _____

4 _____

  _____

5 _____

  _____

6 _____

  _____

7 _____

  _____

8 _____

  _____

9 _____

  _____

10 _____

  _____

11 _____

  _____

12 _____

  _____

13 _____

_____

14 _____

_____

15 _____

_____

2   Action check

On Side two of the audio cassette, you will hear a number of people speaking in various marketing situations. Listen carefully to the extracts, and try to answer the questions.

Write your answers and comments in the space below.

Situation 1: _____

_____

_____

_____

_____

_____

Situation 2: _____

_____

_____

_____

_____

_____

Situation 3: _____

_____

_____

_____

_____

_____

Situation 4: _____

_____

_____

_____

_____

_____

_____

| 3 | Unit assessment |

Time guide 60 minutes

Read the following case incident and then deal with the questions which follow, writing your answers on a separate sheet of paper.

Case Study

Recorded music has long been available on vinyl LPs and audio cassettes. In recent years, Compact Discs (CDs) have been introduced, and this new product has taken an increasingly large share of the market:

	1984		1990	
	Total sales (millions)	Share of market (%)	Total sales (millions)	Share of market (%)
LPs	54	54%	24	16%
Cassettes	45	45%	74	50%
CDs	0.9	1%	50	34%

The market is changing with great speed. Although sales of audio cassettes have increased, this part of the market is slowing down. CD sales, on the other hand, are growing fast.

Vinyl LPs seem to be on the way out. In Japan, they are now only sold in a few specialist shops for collectors. In Britain, the consumer electrical industry believes that before long, hi-fi systems will usually come without LP turntables. This is despite the fact that CDs are more expensive than the equivalent vinyl LP.

Suppose you are a supervisor in a factory which mainly specializes in pressing vinyl LPs, with a smaller operation duplicating audio cassettes.

This is a change in the market with important implications for the people in the workteam – and for their supervisors. Think about the issues carefully, and then write down detailed notes which would enable you to answer the following questions:

1. What is the short-term effect on the people who work in the firm likely to be, and how should the supervisors handle it?

2. What can the firm do to try and predict whether the changes shown in the table above are likely to continue at a similar rate?

3. What measures will the firm have to take if it wishes to stay in the music reproduction business?

4. What will this mean for the workforce in the longer term, and how should the supervisors handle this?

67

Time guide 60 minutes

The time guide for this assignment gives you an approximate idea of how long it is likely to take you to write up your findings.

You will need to spend some additional time gathering information, perhaps talking to colleagues and thinking about the assignment. The result of your efforts should be presented on separate sheets of paper.

Even if you don't deal with the customer face to face, you may have contact in writing or on the telephone. You almost certainly contribute to a product or a service which, ultimately, the customer uses.

Perhaps you feel that you don't have customers at all – especially if your job is providing information or services to other departments in the same organization. But in that case, your customers are the colleagues that you serve: the people who use whatever you provide. Each customer contact is an opportunity to improve the relationship with the customer. Even a complaint, if dealt with correctly and promptly, can improve customer relations.

1. Make a list of all your customer contacts, both internal and external, with a note of the product or service that you supply to them.

2. Choose *five* customers from your list and write down *one* way in which you could improve the service to that customer, so that he or she gets:

   ■ the right product;

   ■ at the right price (if any);

   ■ at the right place;

   ■ at the right time;

   ■ in the right way.

UNIT REVIEW

1   Return to objectives

Now that you have completed your work on this unit, let us review each of our unit objectives.

You should be **better able to:**

- understand what is meant by the market and the marketing approach, and how important they are in the modern world;

We have seen how the ever-changing and highly competitive market is the fundamental fact which determines how businesses operate. The future of every commercial organization, and a good many non-commercial ones, is entirely dependent on success or failure in the market. The most successful organizations are those which understand the need to gear all their activities towards meeting the market's needs. This is the only guarantee of growth, jobs, and indeed survival.

- understand the marketing mix, and how an organization's resources are used to satisfy customers' needs;

The marketing mix means everything that contributes to the marketing effort. It starts with research, and includes the product, the price, the service and everything else, including the promotional and selling effort. In a highly competitive world, any shortcoming in the marketing mix offers an opportunity for a competitor to gain an advantage. Everyone on the payroll contributes to the marketing mix in some way, and everyone therefore shares responsibility for helping the organization's marketing effort.

- adopt the marketing approach and apply it to your everyday activities.

Only you can tell if you have met this objective. My guess is that having worked through the unit, you will by now be starting to apply the ideas we have discussed both personally and with your workteam. Once you have adopted the marketing approach, you will have no shortage of situations in which you can make a positive contribution to the organization's success in the market.

2   Extensions

I recommend that you take up as many of the extensions as you can. They will further increase your understanding and interest, and the extra time and effort will prove very worthwhile.

Extension 1   Book: *Marketing*

Author: R. G. I. Maxwell

Publisher: Macmillan Professional Masters

Extension 2   Book: *Do Your Own Market Research*

Authors: P. N. Hague and P. Jackson

Publisher: Kogan Page

Extension 3

Book: *Advertising*

Author: F. Jefkins

Publisher: Heinemann (Made Simple Series)

Most of this book is about advertising, but it also contains sections on Public Relations, Sales Promotion, and Exhibitions and Trade Fairs.

Extension 4

Book: *How to Turn Customer Service into Customer Sales*

Author: B. Katz

Publisher: Gower Business Skills

This is an American-style book all about selling, and not all of it is relevant to the work of a typical supervisor. However, Chapter 7 on 'Using the telephone' and Chapter 9 on 'Turning complaints into orders' are both useful.

These Extensions can be taken up via your Support Centre. They will arrange for you to have access to them. However, it may be more convenient to check out the materials with your personnel or training people at work – they could well give you access. There are good reasons for approaching your own people as, by doing so, they will become aware of your continuing interest in the subject and you will be able to involve them in your development.